ANALECTA BIBLICA

INVESTIGATIONES SCIENTIFICAE IN RES BIBLICAS

145

ROBERT NORTH, S.J.

THE BIBLICAL JUBILEE

... *after fifty years*

EDITRICE PONTIFICIO ISTITUTO BIBLICO - ROMA 2000

IMPRIMI POTEST

Romae, die 22 martii 2000

R.P. ROBERT F. O'TOOLE, S.J.
Rector Pontificii Instituti Biblici

IMPRIMATUR

Dal Vicariato di Roma, 24 marzo 2000

✠ LUIGI MORETTI
Vescovo tit. di Mopta
Segretario Generale

ISBN 88-7653-145-9
© E.P.I.B. – Roma – 2000
Iura editionis et versionis reservantur

EDITRICE PONTIFICIO ISTITUTO BIBLICO
Piazza della Pilotta, 35 - 00187 Roma, Italia

Table of Contents

Preface

This is not a second edition of our dissertation written in 1950 and published as Analecta Biblica 4 in 1954. We did in fact at once have an interleaved copy bound, in which for thirty years we inserted all the new titles and arresting statements we could find. After editing *Elenchus of Biblica* 1980-95 we caught up pretty well with an apparent reburgeoning of interest. But we abandoned all idea of a second edition, for three reasons.

1. It had never been our intention to publish our results as a dissertation in its entirety as it stood. But Cardinal Augustin Bea, who had been then our highly esteemed Rector and my second *Doktorvater*, recommended it. Proof-correction owed much to the generosity of Père Jean Simon.

2. The title of our dissertation remained "Sociology of the Biblical Jubilee", which seemed to correspond quite well to its contents (it owed much to Max Weber); and indeed as recently as 1993 Gerstenberger used a subtitle *Soziologie des Jobeljahres*. But the "Sociology of" has been abandoned, for two reasons: 1) there seems to be a recent trendy fondness for titles like "Sociology *of* ..." or "Theology *of* ..." as if climbing up on the bandwagon of a more successful and popular research-area; 2) sociological journals from the start totally ignored my volume. Sociologist confreres kindly and convincingly explained to me why this should be. And in fact I signed up in a University sociology department for several courses aimed precisely at clarifying its own self-definition (and distinction from anthropology, no easy matter). More clinching is the fact that several quite recent exegetes, lamenting that sociological methods have been neglected in Bible study and endeavoring to diminish this lack, cite some few starts that have already been made but without including my title (even when it was given approvingly in other areas of their bibliography).

3. There has been a notable change in the outlook of the numerous jubilee-relevant publications of the past decade, and their hermeneutic and socioeconomic base. Just because it is new does not mean that it is right, nor even that it is more interesting. But it seems appropriate to approach the subject anew rather than from viewpoints that were up-to-date fifty years ago. Our entirely reordered Table of Contents may show how we have tried to make the topics more enlivening and captivating than the Contents of 1950.

i

Jubilee

Jubilee is undoubtedly one of the most joyful and expressive words of our languages. Nowadays it usually means the excitement and pleasure felt for a couple who have lived in marriage for 50 years; or for individuals who have spent equally long in a difficult vocation; or for institutions and enterprises that have had a suitably long success.

1. Implications of the Jubilee in its context

But this sense of jubilation is not exactly that of its Semitic origins. It was very early confused with a Latin verb from *jubilus*, the commonplace exulting of simple farmers at the moment of getting in every year's harvest, whether or not it was particularly abundant. Of course this kind of jubilation is not lacking in the context of Lev 25,10, but it is there rather associated with blessings at the expiration of long and very long time-limits.

This is really the only decisive occurrence of *yôbēl* in the Hebrew Bible. We will consider its dozen echoes below, in our effort to determine its etymology. But really the meaning of any word is independent of its linguistic origins, and must be determined by reflection on its contexts. This is ultimately what the dictionary gives us (after a brief parenthesis on its etymology), sifted out and classified from the usages of many centuries.

What Lev 25,10 really describes is a "homecoming" qualifed first as a "release, liberation, *dᵉrôr* (from debt)" and then as a "repossession of land (lost by forced sale)". Our understanding of jubilee as a homecoming is borne out by Weinfeld: *Dᵉrôr*, "*anduraru*, from Sumerian *ama-ra-gi₄*, whose literal meaning is return to the mother ... became a sort of stereotype in the proclamation of 'liberty' up to the Hellenistic period, for we read in the inscription of the famous Rosetta Stone which describes the proclamation of 'liberty' by Ptolemy V in respect to the return of each man to his private holding, *katelthóntas ménein epì tôn idíōn ktéseōn* (OGIS no. 90) and in other proclamations .. regarding the return of a man to his home and family"[1]. But even before these features, the Jubilee is described in terms of *proclaiming* by blowing the *šôpar*-horn "on the tenth day of the seventh month". Seventh month of what? The expression seems to imply that Nisan (March-April) was the *first* month, as in the Ex 12,2 Passover. Presumably it had its own civil or agricultural New Year's Day (nowhere in the Bible a cultic feast). The tenth day of the seventh month is expressly declared to be Atonement-Day (Lev 16), which by later Jewry was put in close relation to their New Year's Day. But there never was among the Hebrews a first month in autumn (Tishri), and the only calendar they ever clearly used (and only after the Exile) was the Standard Mesopotamian of their Aramaic neighbors, beginning in the spring[2].

2. "Sale" regulations qualified by Jubilee

In a certain true sense, the Jubilee-legislation and Leviticus 25 are coextensive. But the chapter is also structured into clearly recognizable sections, and the Jubilee itself occupies only verses 6-13. The rest consists of various related decrees or usages, some earlier and some later. For this reason we will defer a translation of the whole chapter to p.87-91 in our chapter 8 on Source-Dissection, where it will be more useful and needed.

Most immediately linked to the Jubilee are the verses 13-16 regulating or rather qualifying the use of the term "sale". "*Mākar* does not deal with the purchase of cultivable land, as would appear from the usual translations", but here is "transfer of usufruct"; in Jg 3,8; 4,2; 1.7 it is "hand over, deliver (to enemies (for a specified period)"; in general it means "to give away, to deliver" as also in Akkadian (sometimes "in return for valuables" but not

---

[1] Moshe WEINFELD, *Social Justice in Ancient Israel and in the Ancient Near East* (< Hebrew 1985; Jerusalem/Minneapolis 1995, Hebrew Univ./Fortress), p. 159, citing further XENOPHON, *Hellenica* II.4,38; 3 Mcb 7,8, and with ample treatment of *mišarum* (→ p.66), His p. 153 relates Lev 25 to Zedekiah's release of Jer 34,14. -- On *dʳrôr*, Dominique CHARPIN, "L'*andurarum* à Mari", *MARI* 6 (1990) 253-270.

[2] Mark E. COHEN, *The Cultic Calendars of the Ancient Near East* (Bethesda MD 1993, CDL-Press) p. 299-302. -- On the universal economic upset (BOTTÉRO,*Désordre*, p.66 n.24 below): R.K. HARRISON, *Leviticus* (Tyndale OT, 1980) p. 223 says confidently, "The prescribed interruption in the normal course of national life .. would furnish an opportunity for reflection upon covenant values, and remind the nation that man does not live by bread alone".

always expressing reciprocity)[3].

A question that has not been resolved, or indeed hardly ever raised, is whether the (*pro tem*) purchaser has the right to *occupy* the farm, either to supervise the work of the former owner now as his tenant; or to till it himself or with other employees, thus forcing the former owner to find another place to live and work. This last alternative does indeed seem to be borne out by our term "homecoming" which in turn reflects accurately Lev 25,13: at the jubilee he "comes back into possession" of his former plot.

However, through the details of the whole rest of the chapter one has perhaps strongly the impression that it is the former owner who continues to live on the plot as tenant, and must deliver the crop (beyond what his family needs to live on) to the buyer, who lived doubtless in a city. As for the question of whether the buyer may in some cases choose to live on the farm in order to supervise the tenant, there is no hint anywhere in the text of such an arrangement. But insofar as it remains a possibility, or indeed insofar as the defaulting debtor is often presumed to remain as tenant on the same plot of land, the term "homecoming" of Lev 25,13 would correspond less well to the rest of the chapter.

We note below a suggestion unusual or even unique in exegesis. The so-called "sale", with a jubilee restitution far off in a future in which likely enough both parties will be dead (and meanwhile the unrealized "gô'el-repurchase" always in the wings), was a kind of "casuistry" whereby the requirement of Lev 25,23 could be "circumvented". Though not formally or legally the owner, the "buyer" was really owner for all practical purposes[4].

3. Debated practicality of the jubilee duration

A major concern of all commentators has been whether the jubilee was a real law, intended to be obligatory whether it was ever actually observed or not (though that is also a problem, as will have to be discussed under "historicity" below, ch.9), or whether it was just a pious homily, an earnest exhortation, a utopian eschatological dream-hope.

The "utopian" view is largely linked to a late exilic dating of the

---

[3] Edward LIPIŃSKI, "Sale, Transfer, and Delivery in Ancient Semitic Terminology", in Horst KLENGEL, ed., *Gesellschaft und Kultur im alten Vorderasien*: Schriften zur Geschichte und Kultur des Alten Orients 15 (Berlin 1982, Akademie; 173-185) 175; 178; 184.
[4] Eryl W. DAVIES (→ p.35n5), his p. 360.

Jubilee (or of the whole chapter), which probably is somewhat more common among commentators, often linked with Isa 61 or with the return from exile, as we discuss below[5]. A solution for the utopian implausibility of a simultaneous (fallow and) land-ownership change all over the country has been suggested in the possibility that the blowing of the trumpet was like a "registering of deeds" or public official acknowledgment of the legitimacy of changes just beginning to take place over a longer period of time[6].

Those who maintain a historical reality, if not of Lev 25,10 itself, then at least of an earlier tradition which it retrieves, have generally found that the likeliest historical period for the emergence of such a tradition was the time of the settlement attributed to Joshua, when Israel's hopes were high and the fulfilment was so far off as not to seem implausible[7].

The "50 years duration" scheduled to intervene before regaining the land lost by debt is given as a maximum[8]. The detailed regulations imply that it would in most concrete cases have been less than that. If a farmer fell into his debt-crisis only 20 years before the Jubilee, say at the age of thirty, he could look forward to a real advantage in regaining title to his property at the age of fifty: though to be realistic we should recognize that in the meantime his work-days would be spent pretty much just as before and after.

Amid the very detailed regulations, nothing is really said to determine exactly how much or what percentage of the harvest is to be turned over annually by the tenant-debtor to the *pro tem* "owner" (leaving out of account the minority view that it was the "owner" and not the debtor to whom would accrue the actual working of the land). There is indeed a very slight hint in Lev 25,26 (among the several ways in which the land might be regained even before the Jubilee) that the ex-owner might manage this himself by a capital which he had meanwhile procured: "how ?" is not said. But the exegetes suggest that it might have been an inheritance, or it might also have been due

---

[5] See p.97 & 117-9; more utopian is Gerhard WALLIS, "Das Jobeljahr-Gesetz, eine Novelle zum Sabbathjahrgesetz", *Mitteilungen des Instituts für Orientforschung* 15 (1969) 337-345.

[6] David L. LIEBER, "Sabbatical Year and Jubilee", *Encyclopaedia Judaica* 14 (1971; 574-577) p. 576, approving R. NORTH, *Sociology of the Biblical Jubilee*: Analecta Biblica 4 (Rome 1954) p.173.

[7] Martin NOTH, *Das dritte Buch Mose, Leviticus*: Altes Testament Deutsch 6 (Göttingen 1962, Vandenhoeck & Ruprecht) p. 185 holds that the Jubilee land-restoration decree could go back to the Joshua-era, but that the frame came from the exilic period before Lev 23,24, where the trumpet for the cultic sabbath is on the first and not the tenth of the seventh month; so HARTLEY, Leviticus 425.

[8] E. STONE, "The Hebrew Jubilee Period", *Westminster Review* 175 (1911) 686-696.

to especially good crops some years. This would imply, though rather tenuously, that the ex-owner working the land as tenant was obliged to hand over, leaving out what had been needed for his family's sustenance, only a *part* of the surplus, keeping the rest to build up a little capital for himself.

These factors, though all very dubious and vague, must be taken into account in evaluating Cortese's otherwise rather interesting solution given below in ch.8 as to when and how the specific "50 year Jubilee" would most likely have been inserted into the biblical text. He says harshly that a delay of 50 years would have been "ridiculous and cruel" for any actual farmer, but does double-duty for indicating also a likely duration of the Exile soon to end with the restoration of *all* the returnees' land. He might well have gained his essential goals by indicating how a less "ridiculous and cruel" delay than 50 years is actually envisioned in the text for some or most cases.

Gnuse's position here may perplex. He begins by extolling the jubilee "legislation" as an unsurpassed vision of social and economic reform, for which earlier legal sources are given and the subordinate obligations are debated. Only with "the mechanics of the jubilee" are refuted one by one all positions except that of a "vision of hope, inspiring still today; an 'institution' which may never have existed in historical reality"[9]. His observations might have carried more weight if he had begun with this statement and then set forth the detailed elements of the jubilee not as regulations or laws but as the organized formulation of such a "pious hope".

4. Fiftieth as 49th year or 49-day intercalary

A rare rabbinical commentary (Judah bNed 61a) maintained that the Jubilee year is really the forty-ninth or seventh sabbatical, as plainly stated in Lev 25,8-9; but is called "fiftieth" in Lev 25,10 as including the preceding jubilee year. My 1954 ch.5 in discussing other possibilities maintained rather, with many or most commentaries, that 50 was a "round number" for 49. But I now have to point out the justice of Lemche's observation (ftn.16, his p.47) that in a Semitic counting-system in which "seven" was so important, 49 had just as much right to be considered a "round number". Even so, the rabbinic solution making the 50 include the preceding Jubilee has been fairly widely accepted since Kugler ($\rightarrow$ p. 26n17).

A strictly "50th" year would seem to be supported in Lev 25,22 by

---

[9] Robert GNUSE, "Jubilee Legislation in Leviticus; Israel's Vision of Social Reform", *BTB* 15 (1985) (43-) 48.

unexpected mention of a "ninth" year involved as following a double fallow, 49th (= 7th 7th) and 50th (= 8th), for which God's special blessing will give in the 6th produce enough for three years (Lev 25,21). But these verses seem to refer explicitly to the ordinary every-7th-year fallow ("you will sow the 8th year", Lev 25,22), whose pinch would still be felt in the second year following (→ p. 26).

Efforts to make 49th equal 50th are also based on alleged references to concurrent calendars, one (civil? beginning in spring, Nisan, Ex 12,2; implied also in Lev 25,9) and another (religious; postbiblical New Year in autumn, Tishri). Assyrian and Hebrew calendars are also reckoned with[10].

But doubtless the most intriguing effort has been that of Zeitlin to make the "49th year" an intercalary of only 49 days, as an approach to diminish the known discrepancy between lunar and solar year (→ p.27n21). "The most viable solution has been offered by Hoenig, who suggests that the *yôbel* was a very short "year" only 49 days long, intercalated in the seventh month of the forty-ninth year. This adjustment was necessary [though insufficient] to bring the Jewish calendar in line with the solar year. However, such a theory requires that the Massoretic Text be amended to read 49 days instead of 49 years"[11].

5. Etymology of "Jubilee"

In the Septuagint Greek translation *yôbēl* is regularly rendered *áphesis* "release", which is also the sense of *dᵉrôr* (*andurārum*, liberation) used as synonym or rather definition of "jubilee" in Lev 25,10. Moreover the frequent Hebrew verb *yābal* means "to bring, proceed" but in contexts implying a somewhat solemn fashion. The form *yᵉbûl*, which would seem to be derived from the same verb though not so indicated in the Gesenius-Brown dictionary, is also frequent for "products of the soil", vaguely even if

---

[10] Julius LEWY, "The Biblical Institution of *Dᵉrôr* in the Light of Akkadian Documents", *Eretz-Israel* 5 (Fest. B. MAZAR) *21-*31; p. *30, "no evidence to show that also non-Israelite legislators advocated the connection of the general releases with the 'jubilee'" [but p. *29:] the ancientness of such injunctions proves the pre-monarchic origins of Lv 25,10.

[11] Sidney B, HOENIG, "Sabbatical Years and the Year of Jubilee", *JQR* 59 (1969) 222-236; Gregory C. CHIRICHIGNO, *Debt-Slavery*: JSOT supp. 141 (1993) 319: but he concludes that the text assumes 50th for 49th, a "heightened" sabbath year, as NORTH & CARDELLINI.

not directly relevant to Lev 25[12].

The origins of *áphesis* bear comparison with those of *yábal*: *híēmi* means "to send" + *apò* "to send off, let go". Carmichael in a long footnote (without even mentioning the "ram") strongly supports our link of *híēmi* especially with *y^{e}bûl*, "abundant crops" in Lev 26,4.20[13].

However. the Hebrew dictionaries and concordances give (as an entirely different word unconnected with either *yábal* or *y^{e}bul*) a word *yôbēl* in a list of sacrificial animals, presumably meaning "ram" (in the Phoenician Marseilles Tariff discovered only in 1853) given in Hebrew "only in the combination 'ram's *horn*'" -- meaning really horn plus usually several further qualifiers, as we will note. As a curiosity may be metioned a "prophetic anticipation" of *yôbēl* as rare synonym of *dikra*,"horn" (Bartenora citing Aqiba).

Five biblical occurrences of *yôbel* are at the beginning of Joshua 6, in the ritual *t^{e}rû'â*, "hornblowing, blast"[14]. My 1954 book does not seem to have noted that Gesenius-Brown credits to a single root-word not only all these occurrences of *yôbel*/"ram" in Joshua plus Leviticus 25 & 27, but also Ex 19,13 and Num 36,4. But neither could I notice that in the 1958 Concordance of Gerhard Lisowsky only the Joshua and Exodus items are credited to "ram or horn"; the others are put separately as "release-year".

It was undoubtedly a stern warning when virtually all scholarly reviews and other early citations flatly rejected my linking Jubilee with *áphesis* instead of with the Phoenician ram. This judgment may perhaps be traced in two ways to W.F. Albright, to whom I, as all the exegetes of my generation, am deeply indebted and grateful for the insertion of updated archeology into exegesis. His authority became so great that it was natural in judging any new proposal or thesis to try to ascertain whether Albright (or his "school": Wright, Anderson, Bright ..) had expressed a judgment, in order to conform to it, or more rarely to attain fame by disproving it.

A second trend, this time of Albright himself, was whenever any new excavated information appeared, to utilize it immediately for solving long-

[12] Exceptionally, S. H. HIRSCH, *The Pentateuch* (1962) 739 [cited by G. ROBINSON (p.120n12, her p.493] supports our linking *yôbel=áphesis* with the Hebrew verb *yábal*, and even claims the Phoenician *ybl* (sacrificial animal; ram) is a "popular" (rather than "scholars'") etymology.

[13] Calum CARMICHAEL (→ p. 22, ftn.7), his p. 232, citing N.P. LEMCHE, "Manumission", *VT* 26 (1976: ftn.16 below), his p. 50 ftn. 36 discussing *biltu,*

[14] Paul HUMBERT, *La Terou'a. Analyse d'un rite biblique.* Neuchâtel 1946.

standing exegetical cruces in place of the stodgy solid old philology; Phoenician has more appeal than Septuagint. I recognize these values in the judgment of Albright and am grateful to him as a help for me as well as for scholarship. And I deplore the recent storm of attacks on his aims and his methods, to the extent that recent critics regrettably can toss off "That's as bad as Albright".

But the fact is that more recently there has been a modest tendency to show cautious interest in my *áphesis*. I would now more open-mindedly say that there are two possibilities open, *áphesis* and ram, each with its merits[15]. Nevertheless I still feel it may be ironical but is not unfair to say with Klostermann that in choosing "ram" we are really choosing "ram(s'-horn-blast-inaugurated-release-year)". Not that it would be difficult to find even more far-fetched etymologies.

Among the recent exegetes favoring, at least as possible alternative, my *áphesis* are Lemche and Carmichael cited above[16]. Kutsch in RGG[3] flatly favors *ybl* (Akkadian *biltu*, "bring gifts"), not "ram"[17].

Stephen Kaufmann grants "the etymology of *yôbēl* is uncertain" in (Num 36,4) as part of his rather sweeping claim that it is disconcerting "to see that scholars who should know better regularly confound the fallow year with the sabbatical year and think of the Jubilee (*yôbel*) as a year-long period instead of a point in time"[18].

A special attention, not particularly etymological, is shown by Sharon Ringe's observation in our ch. 10 below (p.119,ftn.10, her p.34) that whereas

[15] A. VAN SELMS, "Jubilee, Year of" in *IDB* supplement (1976) 196, holding the *yᵉbûl* etymology improbable, notes (*qrn*) *hybl* as a musical instrument in Ex 19,13 and Jos 6,5; but regarding Jos 6,4.6-13 he cites Mishnah RH 3,5 (ram's horn used only for New Year) and 3,3 (the straight goat-horn was prescribed for the jubilee).

[16] N.P. LEMCHE, "Manumission ..", *VT* 26 (1976) 41: his favor for *yābal*-etymology does not compare *áphesis* but Akkadian *biltu* "though (!) this was rather for soil-products"; MEINHOLD *TRE* 17 (1988) 280 rather Akkadian *yabilu* "wether"; H.A. HOFFNER *TDOT* 5 (1986) 565 < *ThWAT* 3 (1982) 391 derives *yᵉbûl* from Akkadian *bl* "flood" and compares Phoenician ram with Akkadian *yabilu* as "sheep, ram" without mentioning jubilee (TDOT 6,2).

[17] E. KUTSCH, "Jobeljahr", *Die Religion in Geschichte und Gegenwart*[3] 3 (Tübingen 1960) 799 [*RGG*[4] 1 (A-B) appeared in 1998].

[18] Stephen KAUFMANN, "A Reconstruction of the Social Welfare Systems of Ancient Israel", in Fest. G.W. AHLSTRÖM, *In the Shelter of Elyon*, ed. W.B. BARRICK & J.R. SPENCER: JSOT supp. 31 (Sheffield 1984; 279-286), p. 285; 278. His p. 280 notes that 7 years is too seldom for fallow.

"in Hebrew, Jubilee traditions are marked by a special vocabulary [d^erôr, yôbēl], in Greek the vocabulary is not distinctive ... in LXX Lev 25:10 and elsewhere, both of these Hebrew words are rendered by the common word *áphesis*, which has a broad range of meanings beyond the Jubilee traditions". Among the important consequences she draws is that the Gospel authors themselves did not know when they were citing an OT jubilee reference; from the Greek words that are used, it is difficult for her to decide which phrases of the Jesus tradition are also and ultimately part of the Jubilee tradition.

6. Focus on the small (independent then sold out) farmer

It is usually (perhaps 100% of the cases) maintained or supposed that the biblical Jubilee institution and chapter was intended as an overall social reform, whether as law or only ideal to be striven for. We must now seriously question that assumption.

Upon careful re-reading, it will be seen that the Jubilee chapter is interested solely in the small independent farmer and in helping him to remain such. Everything that is said about debt, usury, slavery, repurchase, and even cultus has only this is mind. Moreover what is envisaged is not the small farmer as a person with his wants and needs, but only the goal of keeping Israel's property united in the families to which it was assigned at the "outset". Curiously this "entailing" of landed property so that it will remain always in the important families, though to some extent it could have impeded (non-Go'el: p.45) latifundism, was precisely one of the abuses most envisioned by the "social reform" movements of recent centuries.

A more general "poor relief" may be seen in the consequences of the fallow, not really as these are mentioned in Lev 25,7 (though this does mention alien and settler on a par with domestics and livestock), but as fairly clearly preserved from Ex 23,11 though precisely without the phrase "so that the poor among you may eat". Apart from this there is no social reform implied in Lev 25 except in keeping the small farmer's eventual ownership.

I must confess that I never recognized this "important family" focus of Lev 25 in my 1954 book, which is really not so surprising if it is never mentioned in any of the hundreds of other writings on this subject. But I may also add that even in preparing this volume it dawned on me only gradually. Now, however, I consider it to be unmistakable.

Even in this, however, I see that one reserve must be added. Insistence on the independent farmer as focus of Lev 25 would apparently imply that (at least its compiler thought that) this was, unless debt intervened, the normal situation for which every farmer and family strove. Upon reflecting more carefully, it would seem likelier that as in most very poor countries the peasants would largely have freely chosen tenancy as a safer way. It may also be that this situation was otherwise at the time of the earlier codes from which Lev 25 organizes and revises the poor-relief laws.

It remains true that the author of the Jubilee chapter carefully gathered together all the fragments of older tradition he could find relating to social justice reforms. He then put them (all of them or perhaps only some which seemed more suitable) into an order relating in some way to the preservation of agricultural property inalienably in the same family in which it had been possessed before. Nothing like fair wages or job security or concern for sickness or old age plays any role in this: overall social justice is not his concern. He is just as little concerned with economical and efficient farming operations (the fallow as he retrieves it or even before was more cultic than practical), or with fair prices and tenant-contracts.

The compiler's major concern is debt, just as it is the major concern of the small farmer trying to keep going. Debt is regarded as slavery; and he interprets the anti-slave traditions he has gathered as one way of dealing with debt. Other ways are loans and the limitation of taking interest on them. Even the cultic is supportive of inalienable property; God is the owner of all, so no change can be made in the manner he has originally chosen for sharing farmland. Despite some few exegetes' or sociologists' efforts, there is no indication of reallotment of plots even within the extended family.

A provisional conclusion may or must be made regarding the date and historical situation in which Leviticus 25 in its definitive form appeared. Though focus on making inalienable the property of the small farmer is not incompatible with the period of "settlement in Canaan" (even taking into account the mammoth revisions of "historicity of the Judges period" since 1950), it seems likely that a new blanket law making all Israel farm property inalienable would better fit the foreseen or recent return from Exile with the hope of claiming for former owners the lands which had been expropriated. But this likelihood must be discussed in more detail below especially in ch.8.

7. Conclusions

Our prized notion of "jubilation" comes really from confusion of a Latin harvest-term with the Hebrew Jubilee. Jubilee means in context "homecoming", equated with *dᵉror* "liberation", and involving a (*šôpar-* ? or *yôbel-*) proclamation on Atonement-Day. This brief notice of Lev 25,8-13 goes on through verse 17 to clarify that chiefly a repossession of indentured property is meant: in the light of which any prior "sale" is restricted.

The decree that this repossession is to take place (apart from some other options) only after fifty years, would have been a not impossible hope during the Joshua settlement for a date so far ahead. But it sounds rather utopian. Hence it is sometimes considered to be "eschatological" as clarified in Isa 61 and Lk 4; or as an exilic invention aimed at the return of former possessions in Judah.

"Fiftieth" here in fact seems to stand for (7 x 7 =) 49th, and thus to eliminate the implausibility of two fallow years in succession. Alternatively it has been taken as an intercalary "year" of only 49 days, not quite enough to make the Jewish lunar year correspond to the solar year.

The etymological origin of "jubilee" is generally taken to be the "ram" of a Phoenician list of sacrificial animals. Thus we would have to understand it as the "ram ('s-horn-blast-proclaimed-release year)". However the Greek *áphesis* by which *yôbel* is generally expressed seems to correspond quite adequately to a native Hebrew root meaning "to send along lavishly" (*híēmi*: with *apò* "away" amounting to "release").

The brief enunciation in Lev 25,9-17 is clarified in the rest of the chapter, taking into account parallels in Ex 21 & 23 & Deut 15 & 23. It is thus seen as a summary of older traditional measures for social reform or poor-relief, generally enhanced with a cultic twist.

But when looked at more closely, the whole chapter focuses solely the small independent farmer. What is threatened, or repossessed, is really not so much his own well-being and that of his immediate family, but rather the ownership of his little plot of land which must remain forever as the property of his larger or clan-family.

This factor can be perceived as paramount in the many other regulations to which it at first sight does not seem relevant. Loans "to keep him alive with you" aim really to keep him from having to mortgage or lose his plot of land. The resulting need of working as a peasant (even on his own former land) is seen as a "slavery" from which he ought to be "liberated" by a more prosperous relative, who can "repurchase" the property even long before the Jubilee, so that it will always remain in the same family.

Even the seventh-year fallow, which (the seventh time) is presented as the base of the Jubilee, is now made universal and cultic, and thus even farther than Ex Deut from its likely but inadequate agricultural origins. The growth of walled cities too, and the attribution of some of them to Levites, contain stipulations rather for inalienable family ownership than for social reform or help of the poor.

ii

Fallow

The Jubilee Year is located in detail within a cycle of seven seventh years. This continues immediately -- at least in the perspective of the final compiler -- a seventh year, which verses 2 and 4 specify as a *sabbath* for the Land and for YHWH.

We continue to use "sabbath year", as a fair number of recent writers also do, in order to avoid the academic and "vacation" connotations which "sabbatical" has acquired in English. Interesting is this definition heading a U.S. theological school ad in the London *Tablet* (Oct.30, 1999, p. 1408): "sab-bat´-i-cal, *n.*   A time to replenish your spirit, rejoice in your accomplishments, and re-imagine your work". But we would not question the dependence of such modern definitions on the Old Testament initiative.

1. Seven as a significant number in the Ancient Near East

Perhaps only Cardellini shows doubt that the Jubilee was in itself intended as a heightening of the seventh sabbath year[1]. At the opposite end of the spectrum, Alt held that the Jubilee legislation was originally intended for *every* seventh year[2].

---

[1] Innocenzo CARDELLINI, "Le radici del 'Giubileo' biblico", *Seminarium* 31 (1999; 36-62; bibliog. 63-72) p. 54; p. 61 adds that "because of its absurdity [totalizing view of the world]" the Jubilee had either fallen into disuse by the time of Nehemiah or had not yet been instituted (historically; more likely it was just a narrative to celebrate the liberation by Cyrus 538). P.P. SAYDON, "Leviticus" in *A New Catholic Commentary on Holy Scripture*. ed. R.C. FULLER, *al.* (London 1969, Nelson; 228-241) p. 240, though starting out Lev 25 with "The Sabbatical Year and the Year of Jubilee [were] two different institutions which at certain times coincided" says under Jubilee, "based on the same principle of a period of seven time-units".

[2] Albrecht ALT, *Ursprünge* 1934 [p. 61, ftn.2 below], English cited by FAGER 1993 [p.37n7] as p. 164 (1966 ed.?), but in the JSOT 1989 reprint it is p. 128. According to REVENTLOW [ftn. 17 below], p. 124, Wellhausen also held that the present Jubilee-enactments were intended originally for every seventh year; but he defends against Wellhausen JIRKU's view (p.171) that the jubilee was not postexilic but a very ancient tradition.

"Seven" itself, even if not clarified as "sabbath (day/year)" is claimed to have a sacrality of its own, and to have been used at Ugarit in this sense more often than in its numeric-literal sense[3]. But we will not follow up here our research on the origins of sabbath, except to note some important treatments which have meanwhile appeared[4].

Gordon makes an interesting observation perhaps nowhere else noticed. The Hebrew names of the first six days are simply their number, to reject both the Latin and Germanic naming of them from pagan gods; but for the seventh day *šabbetai* was retained because prehistorically Saturn was their protector deposed by Jupiter[5].

With its various sevens, the Joseph story, Gen [41,44-55] 47,18-27, is seen by Skinner as "aetiological. The Hebrews were impressed by the vast difference between the land-tenure of Egypt and that under which they themselves lived [apparently assuming that the Lev 25 laws were observed]"; the Joseph-story comparison is also in Levine and Wenham "but without explaining why"[6].

Carmichael's added explanation and parallelism is detailed[7]. "In formulating a law about some matter [here: every seventh year the land experiences famine-like conditions not brought on by nature], the biblical lawgiver typically turns to a first-time occurrence of a problem in the

---

[3] Arvid S. KAPELRUD, "The Number Seven in Ugaritic Texts", *VT* 18 (1968; 404-9) p.408.

[4] R. NORTH, "The Derivation of Sabbath", *Biblica* 36 (1955) 182-201; Roland DE VAUX, *Ancient Israel* (London 1962) 475-482; Felix MATHYS, "Sabbatruhe und Sabbatfest", *ThZ* 28,4 (1972) 241-262 (fasc. 3 also has duplicated pages 241-256); Klaus KOCH, "Sabbatstruktur der Geschichte. *Die sogenannte Zehn-Wochen-Apokalypse (1 Hen 93,1-1; 91,11-17) und das Ringen um die alttestamentlichen Chronologien im späten Israelitentum", ZAW* 95 (1983) 403-430; Mayer GRUBER, "The Source of the Biblical Sabbath" [not Babylon]", *JANES* 1,2 (1969) 14-20; Florencio MEZZACASA, "Esdras, Nehemías y el año sabático", *Revista Bíblica* 23,99 (1961) 1-8 . 22-96.

[5] TACITUS, Histories 2,5; Cyrus H. GORDON, "The Biblical Sabbath: its Origin and Observance in the Ancient Near East", *Judaism* 31 (1982; 12-16) 15; see also his "Sabbatical Cycle or Seasonal Pattern", *Orientalia* 23 (1952) 79-81.

[6] J.B. SKINNER, *Genesis*: International Critical Commentary (Edinburgh (1910) 501; Baruch A. LEVINE, *Leviticus*: Torah Commentary (Philadelphia 1989, Jewish Publication Society) 272; G.J.WENHAM, *Genesis 16-50*: Word Commentary 2 (Dallas 1994) 448.

[7] Calum CARMICHAEL, "The Sabbatical/Jubilee Cycle and the Seven Year Famine in Egypt", *Biblica* 80 (1999) p.224-239; see also his "the Story of Joseph and the Book of Jubilees" in *The Dead Sea Scrolls in their Historical Context*. ed. T.H. LIM, *al.* (Edinburgh 1999).

nation's history to see how it was resolved. ... There are in fact seven successive years of famine in Egypt [threatening but not producing starvation] ...

"There are, however", Carmichael continues, "economic and social upheavals brought about by the famine [Gen 47,18 two-year climactic period:] all the Egyptians lose their private landholdings, which become the property of their king, and they also become permanent slaves to him. [In Lev 25] the Year of Jubilee produces its own parallel to the second year of the climactic two-year period in Joseph's Egypt ... major social and economic changes ... all Israelites are to return to their ancestral holdings and all Israelite slaves are to be freed ... outcome in striking contrast to the Egyptian situation".

Other details are added: Lev 25,42.55, the Israelites became slaves to YHWH when he brought them out of Egypt. In Lev 25,23, "the land belongs to YHWH" but in Egypt to the pharaoh. As the Levites in 25,34, the Egyptian priests retain their land, Gen 47,22.26. In sum, as Lev 18,3 prescribes, "After the doings of the land of Egypt, wherein ye dwelt, shall ye not do".

Though the Jubilee is joyous, it is proclaimed on Atonement Day (Lev 25,9; p. 234). because this recalls a crucial moment (Gen 45,1-15; 50,15-21): Joseph's reconciliation with his brothers. -- Lev 26,3-5 and 27,17-24 further specify the differing arrangement between supreme authority and subject (p.235). Finally in the dreams of the Joseph story (Gen 40.13), caused by and not causing the corresponding history (p.238), are found what Weinfeld calls "idealistic-utopian elements"[8].

2. Fallow for "the Poor" as Ex 23,11 ?

In the seventh year, Lev 25,3-5 clarify that there shall be neither sowing nor reaping, nor the usual care for the vineyard: in other words, a strict fallow. Verse 6 adds a rather mild hint of poor-relief. This is an echo of the rather stronger Ex 23,11, which is apparently here adapted[9].

---

[8] Moshe WEINFELD, *Social Justice in Ancient Israel* (Jerusalem 1995) 127; on p. 172 he holds, "The biblical laws of the jubilee year thus incorporate Near Eastern legal institutions of great antiquity".

[9] Eberhard H. VON WALDOW, "Social Responsibility and Social Structure in Early Israel", *CBQ* 32 (1970) 182-209; his text promptly makes clear that the title means "for the poor and underprivileged"; p. 183 on Ex 21-23; p.197 on Deut 15 (more strongly for the poor, though without fallow, and with a mild disparity which has been noticed in verse 11, "the poor will

The spontaneous growth of the land is to provide (presumably along with the carefully rationed preceding year's crop) "food for your slaves and tenants" on the same basis as for the owner's family. But nothing is said even in verse 6 about this spontaneous growth being specially for "the Poor".

It is inevitably debated whether the fallow seventh year of Ex 23,10 is the same as the fallow seventh seventh (or, or also) the eighth (Fiftieth) of Lev 25,8.10. In Ex 23,10-12 a strict seventh year fallow is or had been described in almost identical terms. But it includes the verb *tišmᵉtenna*, "you shall release": root of the noun *šᵉmittâ* used distinctively in Deut 15 for two kinds of poor-relief without including any fallow or "sabbath of the Land".

As in Deut 15,12, the seventh year is (also) to be occasion for the freeing of any Hebrew slave in Ex 21,2. "The Priestly author is interested solely in the sacral aspects of the seventh year, while the author of Deuteronomy is interested solely in its social aspect ... it is a 'release of debts ... so that there be not among you a poor man'; it is not a 'release of the land'"[10].

In both cases "after six years" makes it explicit that the liberation is to come separately for each slave's own servitude (unless he has freely committed himself forever by the primitive ear-piercing ceremony of both Ex 21,6 and Deut 15,17). There is no hint of a simultaneous universal release such as we shall see controverted on Lev 25,40 in chapter 6 below.

In Deut 15,1-3, not after six but "after seven years" there is to be a Shemittah. This term means "a release" generally taken to mean "of debts". But there is intense disagreement as to whether this means that the debts are merely "suspended" for a year (which again might mean various things; but if not "interest" for that year, then what, exactly?) or whether the debts are completely canceled[11]. The verses 4 to 14 (shemittah only in verse 9) are

---

never be lacking in your land"); p. 199 on Lev 25. -- William MORROW, "The Composition of Deut 15:1-3", *Hebrew Annual Review* 12 (1990) 115-131; Richard J.COGGINS, "The OT and the Poor", *Expository Times* 99 (1987s) 11-14: in general the biblical writers were upper-class and regarded riches as a good, but they called themselves "poor" -- before God.

[10] Moshe WEINFELD, *Deuteronomy and the Deuteronomic School* (diss. Jerusalem 1964; Oxford 1972) p. 224, 223. On p. 153 n.1 he insists from the *mišārum* and *andurārum* data that against current opinion the jubilee provisions reflect "very ancient tribal reality", which he seems to take unduly to mean that the overall structure of Lev 25 is "not post-exilic"

[11] Christopher J.H. WRIGHT, "Sabbatical Year", *AnchorBD* 5 (1992; 857-861), p. 859 holds that the shemittah was only "suspension" of the debt for one year; p. 858 that since the fallow was for the poor it varied in year for the various fields and was not universal as in Lev 25,4.

rather a homily on helping the poor, and to this extent link up with verses 12-18 despite the differences; and these verses on slave-release are also sometimes called shemittah.

"The cancellation of debts ... as part of the sabbath year code" or more properly as part of the various sabbath year codes, is to be assumed as part of the Jubilee heightening, says Sloan; but this is not generally agreed or expressed, and ultimately must be justified from Josephus[12].

3. Fallow for "the Land itself" or for YHWH ?

The formulation of the Sabbath *Šabbaton*, "Repose, Big Repose" of verse 4, "the Land shall have total rest as a sabbath for YHWH", combines two factors. One is repeatedly stated to be the acknowledgment of YHWH's ownership of the land. The other more elusively implies that the Land has the same right to periodic rest as men and animals, though doubtless few would go as far as Pedersen, "We know that the Israelites do not acknowledge the distinction between the psychic and the corporeal. Earth and stones are alive, imbued with a soul"[13].

This "right" of the land to rest is most explicitly stated in 2 Chr 36,21: "The earlier historical books are silent about the fallow year, but the Chronicler regards the seventy years' captivity and desolation of the land as making up for the unobserved Sabbaths of the land, 'to fulfil the word of the Lord by the mouth of Jeremiah'"[14]. Jeremiah 25,11 and 29,10 say only "70 years (these nations will be captives of the king) of Babylon", without mention of sabbath or sabbath year. Hence Nodet claims that we have here a creation of the Chronicler, echoed in Lev 26,34, "Then the Land will regain its lost sabbaths ['years' not specified] while it is untilled, enjoying that rest which you would not let it have on the sabbaths when you lived there"[15]. Doubtless "sabbath 'years'" may be supposed here in view of the fact that in

---

[12] SLOAN, *Favorable Year* 1977 [p.117n6 below], p. 8; JOSEPHUS, *Antiquities* 3,12,3 (WHISTON Grand Rapids edition p.81).

[13] Johannes PEDERSEN, *Israel, its Life and Culture* 1-2 (1926) 470; the citation is continued in my AnB4 p.113; citing also V. APTOWITZER, "The Rewarding and Punishing of Animals and Inanimate Objects", *HUCA* 3 (1926) 117-155.

[14] Raymond WESTBROOK, *Property and the Family in Biblical Law*: JSOT.supp 113, 1991 [< *Israel Law Review* 6 (1971) 210] and note p. 45 & 66 on *mišarum* of ch. 6.

[15] Étienne NODET, *A Search for the Origins of Judaism, from Joshua to the Mishnah* [*Essai sur les origines du Judaïsme* 1993],tr.E.CROWLEY:JSOT supp.248 (Sheffield 1997) 349.

the Bible there is seldom a hint that the sabbath *day* repose was not observed on the farms.

4. Seventh Sabbath and intercalary 49-day "year"

Regarding our earlier claim for "fiftieth" as just a round number for forty-ninth, we now agree with Lemche that in the biblical numerical system any "seventh" is just as likely to serve as a round number, or more so[16]. Many follow the solution of Rabbi Judah in the Talmud Ned b61a (but not by other rabbis): "fiftieth = 49th plus preceding jubilee"[17].

But the main objection to a 50th year jubilee as distinct from a 49th (sabbatical) remains the difficulty of a two-year universal fallow. Precisely this question of a two-year (universal) fallow is taken up in verse 20. But it there has the appearance of an insert, because the preceding verses have somewhat the solemnity of a conclusion to the original Jubilee passage itself[18]. Still, verse 21 speaks of divinely-increased produce enough for "three" years, and verse 22 alludes to a "ninth" year[19].

Not offering any solution, it is true, but a quite relevant philological curiosity, is Snaith's observation that the spontaneous growth of a *second* year has a different word in Hebrew (*saḥîš* 2 Kgs 19,29; Isa 37,30)[20]. The word for (first-year) growth reserved for the poor in Lev 25,3 (and Kgs Isa)

---

[16] N.P. LEMCHE, Manumission [above p.13 (p.15n16)], p.47. SEIDL LTK³ says flatly that the Jubilee was 7x7=49th year (as my 1954 book and commonly) but he adds more tentatively, as WRIGHT *AnchorBD* 1025 "50th; some scholars say 49th" and that Lev 25,10 in calling it 50th is simply including the preceding jubilee year.

[17] S.M. LEHRMANN, "Book of Leviticus", *Soncino Chumash* (1947), p. 767; A. VAN SELMS, "Jubilee", *IDB supp.* (1976), p. 496(-8). though he himself prefers the parallel "Christ rose on 3d i.e. 2d day". -- Henning G. REVENTLOW, *Das Heiligkeitsgesetz formgeschichtlich untersucht*: WMANT 6 (Neukirchen 1961) p. 125 seems to credit Rabbi Judah's solution rather to F.X. KUGLER, *Von Moses bis Paulus* (Münster 1922, Aschendorff) 17.

[18] Erhard S. GERSTENBERGER, *Leviticus*: ATDeutsch 6 (Göttingen 1993, Vandenhoeck & Ruprecht) p.349: though it is generally admitted that the jubilee-pericope itself (presumably Lev 25,8-23 or 8-17) form the latest full addition to the chapter, in light of which many of the retrieved older laws are adapted.

[19] HARTLEY's Word Comm. *Leviticus* (1992) 437: "The reference to the ninth year is realistic, for [any] sabbatical-year cycle would take a couple of years to recover the supplies depleted during the fallow year, especially given that harvests for different produce come at different times of the year. In this context, the promise, which is primarily for a sabbatical year, may also apply to a year of Jubilee".

[20] N.H. SNAITH., "Leviticus" in *Peake's Commentary on the Bible*, ed. Matthew BLACK & H.H. ROWLEY (London 1962, Nelson; 241-253) p. 252.

is from a root meaning "spill out", *sapaḥ* II, Lev 25,3. But for some Hebraists the overgrowth in Lev 25,11 derives from a *sapaḥ* I "attach".

Several of the more ingenious proposals put forward to account for the disparity beteen 7x7 and 50 are based on the claim that the Jubilee Fiftieth is a short year of only 7x7 days. This view put forward by Solomon Zeitlin in 1929 and refuted by the fact that the "sowing and harvest", autumn and spring/summer, of Lev 25,4 make up a full year, has been taken up and defended by Hoenig. He argues from the fact that the solar year being of only 364 days (instead of 365¼) would then be 49 days behind the seasonal year, enough to constitute an intercalary "year". (Really 61 days would be needed to account for that extra ¼ but it was not known by pre-Ptolemaic astronomers.) Repetition of the prohibition to plant in Lev 25,11 is considered significant specifically for the farmer who has just regained his property but is not allowed to plant it in that brief year (i.e. the end of the current Shemittah). No matter! the real season for planting begins only after the intercalation[21].

This view is taken up by Wenham even in his translation of Lev 23,8 as "You must count seven cycles of sabbatical years; that is, seven years seven times; and the forty-nine days of the seven cycles of sabbatical years shall be for you a year"[22].

Evidence for a similarly shortened fiftieth "year" has been claimed at Qumran[23].

5. Insufficiency of universal seventh-year fallow

The most significant fact involved in the Levitical fallow is the agricultural experience that one year's fallow in seven is not enough; though

---

[21] Sidney B. HOENIG, "Sabbatical Years and the Year of Jubilee", *JQR* 59 (Jan. 1969; 222-236) 232. -- S. ZEITLIN, "The Second Day of the Holidays in the Diaspora", *JQR* 44 (Jan. 1954) 183.

[22] Gordon J. WENHAM, *The Book of Leviticus*: New International Commentary OT 3 (Grand Rapids 1979, Eerdmans) p.314, justified p. 319, where also he admits as "alternative" our *yôbel* = *áphesis*. We appreciate his p.323 using the four points of our theological summary (→ p.115n1). As for his p.318, our "strong case" for a Joshua-era origins of the jubilee, the greatly changed view of early historicity since 1950 (→ below p. 107) will now have to be taken into account.

[23] Annie JAUBERT, "Le calendrier des Jubilés et de la secte de Qumrân. Ses origines bibliques", *VT* 3 (1953) 250; D. CLINES, "Yôbel", *Dictionary of Classical Hebrew* (Sheffield 1998) 4,163 to Qumran in general gives 36 references.

the presumable origin of this tradition in Ex 23,11 leaves open the possibility that not the whole country but each separate plot in turn (or even with crop-rotation on each farm) would have its fallow; in fact only thus would it be of significant help to the poor as prescribed.

Earlier experts are cited for the estimate that the fallow of each plot would have to be at least one year in four. But now one in two -- every other year -- is claimed to need fallow. This strong contention is the main and perhaps only biblical issue really confronted in a book whose actual subject is the title of the Introduction, "The Study of Agriculture in Ancient Israel"[24]. This introduction deplores "not so much how little is known as how little energy has been expended in trying to know".

Since there is really no record of any relevant *facts* before the Greco-Roman era, "method must occupy a preeminent place in any investigation of ancient farming systems". From careful perusal of the contents, I must take this to mean "since we cannot know *what really happened* in biblical-era agricult8ure, we are forced to specify what *must, or might, have happened* from a systematic study of agricultural practice as a whole, chiefly much more recently and far away".

This is not to say that Hopkins gives *no* factual data from the Bible. The very next problem treated after fallow is "fertilization", and many Scripture mentions of the word *dômen*, "dung", are cited; and a few also of how it gets dropped casually on the soil; but we get from these texts, even Jer 9,21, no assurance that the value and need of manure for agriculture were ever recognized in "the highlands of Canaan".

A reference of p. 202 to pp.241-250, instead of the further comments on fallow which we would expect, gives a list of the "seven species" of Deut 8,8 and its total omission of vegetables. Precise data on the (highlands') cereal

---

[24] David C. HOPKINS, *The Highlands of Canaan; Agricultural Life in the Early Iron Age* (Vanderbilt diss. 1983): Social World of Biblical Antiquity Series, 3 (Sheffield 1985, Almond) p. 200. He does not deny that a seventh year *cultic* fallow *also* may have been workable; but he has "avoided the pitfall which has trapped many scholars [all, really! except doubtless DALMAN and REIFENBERG] who, apparently in the absence of any appreciation of agriculture, have taken the sabbatical-year law to describe the totality of agricultural practice in ancient Israel". His data in general are drawn from Adolf REIFENBERG, *The Soils of Palestine; Studies in Soil Formation and Land Utilization in the Mediterranean*[2], tr. C.L. WHITTLES (London 1947, T. Murphy); Gustav H. DALMAN, *Arbeit und Sitte in Palästina* (Gütersloh II. 1932; III. 1935; Bertelsmann); and from unpublished dissertations of Lawrence E. STAGER, *Ancient Agriculture in the Judean Desert: A Case Study of the Buqeiah Valley in the Iron Age* (Harvard 1975) and Oded BOROWSKI, *Agriculture in the Iron Age* (Michigan 1979).

suggested in Amos 4,1 and 1 Chr 27,29-31; also milk, curds, wool in Deut 32,14; 22,11; 2 Sam 17,29; but since "the beasts were themselves a form of capital" (p. 247) meat was rare (1 Sam 14,32). These are the "facts".

A further disturbing factor, not only for Hopkins but also for most of the reported archeological surveys, would be Lemche's claim that there were very few (agricultural) villages in the area treated under "Cities" in ch.7; but there is far wider support for a large number of villages founded at least in the period 1200-1000 B.C.

Stager's study of "agriculture", relying on excavation reports and the Ucko inquiry, gives by millennium the plants cultivated and the animals known to be domesticated in the Canaanite and biblical milieu[25]. The only relevance this can have for our present inquiry would be that the small farmer utilized the cultivation which was known and common in his century.

6. Recorded sabbath years

Recorded actual observance of a fallow seventh year has been sought in post-Biblical testimonies by rabbinic scholars, most recently Wacholder[26]. He does not mention my article on largely the same materials, Maccabees[27], and Josephus. He insists that the observance of Jubilee is nowhere sought by the Rabbis either in or outside the Bible, because it did not constitute a

---

[25] L. E. STAGER, "Agriculture" in *Interpreter's Dictionary of the Bible supplement*, ed. Keith CRIM (Nashville 1978, Abingdon), p. 11-13; D. ZOHARY, "The Progenitors of Wheat and Barley in Relation to Domestication and Agricultural Dispersal in the Old World", p.47-66, & P. DUCOS, "Methodology and Results of the Study of the Earliest Domesticated Animals in the Near East (Palestine)", p.265-275: both in P.J. UCKO & G.W. DIMBLEBY, *The Domestication and Exploitation of Plants and Animals* (1969). See also J. FELIKS, "Agricultural Methods and Implements in Ancient Erez Israel", *EncJud* 2 (1971) 374-382; L. TURKOWSKI, "Peasant Agriculture in the Judean Hills", *PEQ* 101 (1969) 21-33.101-112.

[26] Ben Zion WACHOLDER, "The Calendar of Sabbatical Cycles During the Second Temple and the Early Rabbinic Period", *HUCA* 44 (1973 153-184; tables 185-196. His p. 154 renders Lev 25,4.5 *šabbatōn* as plural, "(of) sabbaths)": perhaps supposed from the apocryphal "Book of (49th year) Jubilees" thereupon-mentioned, citing J. MORGENSTERN, "The Calendar of the Book of Jubilees; its Origin and Character". *VT* 5 (1955) 34-76. See also Wacholder's "Sabbatical Year", *IDB supp* (1976) 762-3, noting Jer 25,11 etc.; Dan 9,24-27 + Enoch; & "Chronomessianism: the Timing of Messianic Movements and the Calendar of Sabbatical Cycles", *HUCA* 46 (1978) 201-218.

[27] R. NORTH, "Maccabean Sabbath Years", *Biblica* 34 (1953) 501-515. See C. H.GORDON, "Sabbatical Cycle or Seasonal Pattern ?" [on A.KAPELRUD], *Orientalia* 22 (1953) 79-81.

calendaric sequence. He also admits that some of the attempted sabbath-year cycles are wrong by a year, and that this was reprehensibly condoned by some rabbinic users.

The main texts are: (1) Neh 10,32, but only promised; and to a law possibly. but less likely, newly made and thus the start of the eight-century cycle. -- (2) Josephus Ant 11,340-5 with his usual hostility to the Samaritans says that Alexander refused to them a sabbath-year tax-exemption which he had granted to the Jews. -- (3) 1 Mcb 6,49 claims famine during instead of after the sabbath-year Beth-Zur siege; Josephus Ant 13,234 makes an *argòn étos* 135/4, which 1 Mcb 16,21 does not qualify as Shemittah. -- (4) Ant 14, 465 & 775 are pressed to make a sabbatical year of 37 B.C.E. in which Herod besieged Jerusalem. -- (5) Milik's Murabba'at II,18 line 1: Nero's Year 2, 55/56 C.E. taken against Milik as the sabbatical year mentioned in line 7; and Murabba'at 24, "precious synchronism between sabbatical and Bar-Kosiba cycles"[28].

Wacholder's "crucial symbol" is the commonly held destruction of the Temple in the month of Ab *following* the sabbatical year 68/69, but amid rabbinic disputations (as hesitantly for Agrippa's reading of Deut 7,15 in post-sabbatical 41/42) Wacholder must turn to Josephus to support his own divergent dating of 69/70 as shemittah, but not 40/41.

The existence of recorded proof for any sabbath year (or Jubilee) pertains further to our ch.9 below on "Historicity".

7. Conclusions

The immemorially venerated "seventh" year appears in Ex 23,11 as a fallow, doubtless somehow related to agriculture, but presented as for the benefit of the poor. In Deut 15,9 also the significance of the seventh year for the poor is stressed, though related to dispossession without mention of fallow. In these cases the "seventh" is likely to have been on varying cycles. But as systematized in Lev 25,4 it is reduced to a universal cycle and "for YHWH" and/or for the right of the Land itself to rest (2 Chr 36,21).

The Jubilee is declared in Lev 25,8 to be a "seventh seventh" year, and in verse 20 to have fully the corresponding character of fallow, though not there declared specially "for the Poor" or "for YHWH". But Lev 25,10 calls the Jubilee "this fiftieth year", not clearly whether during or *after* (Lev 25,9)

---

28 J.T. MILIK, p. 2,125 in (with P. BENOIT, R. DE VAUX) *Discoveries in the Judaean Desert* (Oxford 1961, Clarendon); WACHOLDER, *HUCA* 44 (1973) p.178.

the seventh seventh, i.e. 49th. Verse 22 describes the effects of the jubilee fallow as extending also into a "ninth" (i.e. 51st) year, but it there also speaks perplexingly of "sowing [? not forbidden in] the eighth year".

The dilemma is solved by some exegetes as "50th loosely for 49th" and by perhaps an equal number as "strictly 50th with two fallow years in a row" or else "50th as a shortened or intercalary year".

All these efforts must be seen as mere hair-splitting in view of the recent contention that agriculturally a fallow of all the farm-plots every seven years would do no good at all. It would have to be closer to every second year, and even so in rotation rather than simultaneously. However it is admitted that *alongside* the recurrence of an agriculturally-needed fallow (not mentioned after all in any of the three law-codes cited above), there could have been a separate fallow "for YHWH and/or the Poor". This solution is so recent and revolutionary that no statistic on its acceptance is available.

Even the most ancient Jewish experts most faithful to the Torah admit that the Jubilee year is nowhere recorded as having actually occurred. For the cycle of sabbath years, however, careful records have been kept down to our own day: "careful" rather than "accurate" because they include disputed discrepancies. In any case the "historicity" of the laws either just as laws or in actual observance must depend on a difficult decision as to whether they were really intended as "laws" or as an eschatological or utopian ideal; or possibly as a step toward forcing restoration of farms in Judah after the exile.

iii

Land-Ownership

"The Land is mine, YHWH's" is a key statement on the jubilee. The whole verse Lev 25,23 reads. "The Land shall not be definitively sold, for the Land is mine, and you are but residents (gērîm) who have become my tenants (tôšābîm)." The two Hebrew words had been generally rendered "foreigners" and "aliens", but this emphasis on their origins outside Israel has lately been considered less important than their actual relation to the Land.

1. The Land is the Lord's, but it is for the family

One hardly knows what to make of Ebach's claim that it is not the land but the *people* Israel who form YHWH's *naḥalâ*, "property"; though doubtless this is a way of looking at the social context of YHWH's Land[1].

"The Land is mine" is not to be taken as just a symbol or a metaphor, but as a true statement of fact. And there can be no doubt that for one who believes in creation and God's governance of the universe, God owns all the land not only in Canaan but everywhere, just as he owns the mountains and the seas and the skies and all the rest of creation.

Doubtless this would be admitted even by von Rad in "driving a wedge" between "God owner of the land" (Lev 25,23) as a brand new concept, and the patriarchal view that God is *dispossessing* the "(Canaanite) owners of the land" in order to turn it over to Israel: a "wedge" which Wright contests in

---

[1]   Jürgen EBACH, "Sozialethische Erwägungen zum alttestamentlichen Bodenrecht", *Biblische Notizen* 1 (1976; 31-46) p. 41; on *'aḥuzzâ* as "not conquest but legal acquisition", B. LEVINE, "On the "semantics of Land-Tenure in Biblical Literature (Lev 25,10)", in Fest. W.W. HALLO, *The Tablet and the Scroll* (Bethesda 1993) p. 134-9; F. HORST, "Zwei Begriffe für Eigentum, *naḥalâ* und *'aḥuzzâ*", in Fest. W. RUDOLPH, *Verbannung und Heimkehr*, ed. A. KUSCHKE   (Tübingen 1961, Mohr) p. 135-156; I. CARDELLINI, "'Possessio' [no] o 'dominium bonorum' [yes] ? Riflessioni sulla proprietà privata e la 'remissa dei debiti' in Leviticus 25", *Antonianum* 70 (1995) p. 333-348 [< Gaudium et spes N° 1559]: with so much land uncultivated, we must improve security and favor private initiative; RABINOWITZ Y., "Ba'alut", *Enṣiqlopediya Miqra'ît* 2 (Jerusalem 1954) 295-8.

claiming that both aspects are "sides of the same coin"[2].

In any case it is commonly admitted that in Lev 25 "God's ownership" is used with a special significance in regard to Israel's use of the Land. "Men of the Land and the God of Justice in Greece and Israel" is a comparison which has been made with ample use of Greek data[3].

It seems generally agreed (and obvious) that in Lev 25,23 "God's ownership" means concretely "immutably belonging to the family", but *mišpāḥâ* has recently been taken to mean "extended family (like clan)" rather than one-father family, even to the extent that originally (not hinted in the Bible) the plots were redistributed within it. Thiel maintains that in originally half-nomadic Israel the farmland belonged in principle to the *Sippe*, but there was a a certain amount of *Privatbesitz* apart from the periodically redistributed *Gemeinbesitz*[4] .

It should be stressed here that the insistence on inalienable family ownership of farmland is really the principal object of the Jubilee-chapter Lev 25.

Commentators frequently state that the chapter is a summary of all the social-justice reform traditions of Israel; and this is true in its way. But when looked at under the microscope, it turns out that all the varying proposed reforms regarding debt, enslavement, family relationships, and poor-relief are ultimately in the interest of the inalienability of family property.

It would be more directly evident, though this has hardly ever been noticed by exegetes, that the whole concern of Lev 25 is with the independent small farmer: to preserve him in his ownership despite the menaces of irremediable debt which are a consequence of the risks of weather and health inseparable from a status like his.

---

[2] Gerhard VON RAD, "The Promised Land and Yahweh's Land in the Hexateuch" [< *Zeitschrift des Deutschen Palästina-Vereins* 66 (1943) 191-204] in *The Problem of the Hexateuch and Other Essays* (1966; = Philadelphia/London 1984, Fortress/SCM) 191 (-204); C.J.H. WRIGHT, see *God's People* (1990; p.46 below, n.10) his p. 10.

[3] John Pairman BROWN, "Men of the Land and the God of Justice in Greece and Israel", *ZAW* 95 (1983; 376-403); p. 384, land-tenure crisis; p. 379, crop-rotation. -- Pierre M. PURVES, "Additional Remarks on Nuzi Real Property", *JNES* 6 (1949) 163 ftn. 5 on H. LEWY, *Orientalia* 11 (1942}.

[4] Winfried THIEL, "Die Anfänge von Landwirtschaft und Bodenrecht in der Frühzeit Alt-Israels", in Adelheid BURKHARDT, *al.*, ed., *Altorientalische Forschungen VII*: Schriften zur Geschichte und Kultur des Alten Orients (Berlin 1980, Akademie; 127-141) p.133; 139.

But this concern for the small farmer is not really a personal concern, a humane fellow-feeling for his disadvantages and an aid for him in struggling to overcome them. The ultimate remedy which is proposed would leave him propertiless for a whole lifetime, indeed would commonly not be applicable until after his death. But that is not seen as important, so long as the *principle* of inalienable family property remained intact. In that light, and not merely in view of Isa 61 as Cortese held (p.94 below, n.5) the jubilee solution is not "cruel and ridiculous".

This does not mean that the jubilee-chapter and related older traditions show no sympathetic awareness of the purely personal problems of the small farmer. His risks and disadvantages are tacitly highlighted in all that is said about the unconquerable debt-default which is their consequence.

Nor can we easily agree with Davies' subhead "individual property rights" (rather than "*Family* property rights") or with its claim that the long-deferred jubilee liberation, "whereby the creditor could never become the actual owner of the pledge but could nevertheless use it for his own benefit, was adopted in Israel as a ['casuistic'] means of circumventing the law regarding the inalienability of land (Lev 25,23)"[5]. He in fact admits on the next page that the Jubilee was designed to "preserve the independence of the smaller family unit" and "hinder the development of extensive latifundism".

2. *Varying views of God's vicar as land-owner*

Apart from this fairly clear presentation of the family as his representative in perpetual ownership, God's land-ownership has been taken by both commentators and adversaries to imply a specific ideology of ownership. The Land is God's, yes: but in the sense that here and now its administration belongs to the King as God's representative, or to the Temple priests. Alternatively the Land has been seen as belonging in practice to the conquerors, or to the indigenous inhabitants, or to the competent organizers, or to the poor non-landowners, or "none of the above, just to God alone". These alternatives merit some consideration.

"The Land is Mine: six different land-ideologies" is the title of a very recent and neat little book by Habel. It makes no attempt to reduce to

---

[5] Eryl W. DAVIES, "Land: its Rights and Privileges", in *The World of Ancient Israel: sociological, anthropological and political perspectives*, ed. R.E. CLEMENTS (Cambridge 1989, Univ.; 349-369) p. 360.

a single unity these six views drawn from six different books of the Bible. It also frankly renounces any interest in their historicity or even their legal binding force, but regards each simply as a very original theorizing on the basis of the sad results for Israel's economy from some prevailing uses of the Land for which a better norm is offered. The six views are not unrelated to history, in the sense that they are all drawn from and firmly based on the (nowadays "presumed" or "unprovable") historical context of the books from which they were drawn. But the six ideologies themselves are purely theoretical, not in any sense historical.

Habel's chapter on Leviticus 25 (as an integral unity with 26 and also 27) is entitled "Land as Sabbath Bound: An Agrarian Ideology". This title is shown to mean that Israel is to work the land as tenants (*tôšābîm*) for a (divine; not really absentee-) ownership acknowledged and remunerated by non-working through the whole of every seventh year, and every fiftieth year as well, explicitly declared "supernumerary".

Though unwilling to deal with date of authorship, Habel's book in various casual allusions queries the fairly common view that it is postexilic. At any rate the compiler reinterprets radically the already-existing seventh year fallow laws of Ex 23,11. The fallow is not now for the help of the poor (by rotation of the single fields) but universal over the whole Land as acknowledgment of God's ownership. Stress on the extraordinarily large crop promised in Lev 25,21 to provide for two successive years of universal fallow is hardly needed here for an ideology admittedly purely theoretical.

Account is taken of the fact that this divine ownership is carried through by a division (*nahalah*, "entitlement") of the land-parcels by single families (*mišpᵉḥôt* are clusters of extended families within the tribe; similarity to the Joshua ideology is noted and qualified). But in the end "who benefits from the social order of this land-economy ?" "A stable peasant society", yes; but where does the political power lie ? "The answer, it seems, is with the priests", who "apparently monitor the economic laws of the proposed farm economy" -- by managing the sabbaths and the jubilees[6]. And the "stable

---

[6] Norman C. HABEL, *The Land is Mine: Six Biblical Land Ideologies*: Overtures to Biblical Theology (16). Minneapolis 1995, Fortress. P.111. (On Ex 23, p.102; on the relating of Lev 25 to Joshua, p. 105 & 144). He acknowledges great indebtedness to the editor and first author of the series, Walter BRUEGGEMANN, *The Land* (Philadelphia 1977), but that volume deals rather with the (not economic or agricultural) historical moment of *any* land toward which Israel was successively displaced; only p. 63 mentions "sabbath for freeing slaves (Ex 21), canceling debts (Deut 15) and (later, Lev 25) resting land".

peasantry" is not truly egalitarian: the laborers especially, and all "servants, immigrants, and urbanites".

Beside Joshua, a chapter is devoted to Deuteronomy (nowhere mentioning its ch. 15 shemittah) and another to Jeremiah, notably his ch. 32. Of all six chapters, the first or royal ideology is Solomon's, "the land is for wealth"; and the very last is Abraham's, the only one sympathetic to the indigenous Canaanites (and thus supportive of the author's only prefatory or passing concern for the landless destitute in countries like India and his native Australia).

———

A cognate theoretical approach is shown by Fager's subtitle "Uncovering Hebrew ethics through the sociology of knowledge". A key "slice" through the exilic period of Jubilee growth amasses from vaguely-known history a variety of frankly admitted pure possibilities guided by a Mannheim-inspired mammoth "search for a single principle to explain all phenomena"[7]. More manageable to exegetes will be his noting of Ezek 46,17, which equates with Jubilee the "year of release" (of a "prince's" gift not within his family), giving rise to a whole chapter of similarities and differences between the social-reform approaches of the Jubilee P-compilers and of Ezekiel (who is not noted as being himself a priest).

Also usable will be Fager's mention of a triple purpose of the P compilers: to preserve ancient traditions, explain the exile as a divine punishment, provide proper norms for future living. This is supported by three of the alterations claimed by Ginzberg to have been introduced into the Priestly compilation: (1) originally seventh-year jubilee period lengthened to fiftieth; (2) Deut 15 debt-cancellation suppressed; (4) urban dwellings exempted[8].

3. The King God's vicar as land-owner

As an important factor in determining what is meant by "God's ownership of the land" in the Middle East has long been recognized "the

---

[7] Jeffrey A. FAGER, *Land Tenure and the Biblical Jubilee* [Michigan diss. 1987]: *Discovering Hebrew Ethics through the Sociology of Knowledge*: JSOT supp 155, 1993, p. 39. On p. 52 is P's triple goal; on p. 58 GINZBERG's points; on p. 68, Ezek 46,17 "year of release" = Jubilee.

[8] Eli GINZBERG, "Studies in the Economics of the Bible", *JQR* 22 (1932; 343-408) p. 389.

'King's ownership", surprisingly less extensive than we would infer from absolute sovereignty. The Jubilee-$d^e r\hat{o}r$ cousins *andurarum* and *mešarum* (p. 66 below) are studied chiefly as universal debt-remissions generously granted by the king at some single time near the date of his accession. Such remissions do bear a similarity to the Jubilee, especially for its universality; but also for those like myself who focus its one-time occurrence; or even as an intention plausibly present at its origins, even if difficulties of workability led to a continuous copying of an unenforced law among many similar social-reform ideals which were eventually all organized and solemnized in the magnificently unrealistic itemizings of the Jubilee.

The chief recent study not only of *mešārum* but of all Mesopotamian forms of debt, loan, and release has been Kraus (p.66. n.21-27). It would appear that *mišārum (sakanum)* means literally "(establish) good order", but in concrete cases rather the contrary "*cancel* an existing arrangement" (i.e. debts)[9].

An entirely different aspect of the King as big landholder, but also as enforcer of the divine ethic even against his own interests, is brought to light by Zafrira Ben-Barak. She describes in detail how David's taking over of power from Saul did not automatically include the ex-king's private property. This had in fact been absorbed as public assets simply because the only known heir was too scared to claim it, and was a cripple besides.

But a retainer of Saul and of his heir, with an agenda which turns out to be perhaps not void of self-interest, quite easily induces David not only to restore the property but to take the handicapped heir Meribbaal 2 Sam 9,6 (called also Mephibosheth) generously into his own table-companionship. As a move toward keeping Saul's property within the family, this event is shown to be relevant to convictions underlying not only the Jubilee but the levirate and Naboth[10].

---

[9] F.R. KRAUS, *Ein Edikt des Königs Ammi-ṣaduqa von Babylon*: Studia et Documenta ad Iura Orientis Antiqui Pertinentia 5 (Leiden 1958, Brill) p.44; 242; on *muškēnum*, p. 144; on the reasons for attributing this edict to Ammi-ṣaduqa (first year) p.229 N° 44 (p.106, the formula "17+c" in Ammi-ṣaduqa datings.

[10] Zafrira BEN-BARAK, "Meribaal and the System of Land-Grants in Ancient Israel", *Biblica* 62 (1981; 73-91) 83.

4. What to do when small farming is not efficient ?

The chief alternative to divine land-ownership is latifundia, numerous properties bought up to form a single giant estate of one wealthy owner[11]. Even to hint that "God's ownership" means that the land should be owned by the organizers most competent, seems shamefully to be a commendation of *laissez-faire*. But it would be unreasonable not to give here a lengthier discussion of what our book mentioned briefly as "impractical and uneconomical" small private farming. Surely it could have been made more efficient even within the limits of ancient farm-experience.

Even in the biblical world, for example, we may wonder why there could not have been a moderately cooperative combined ownership. We call this "competent organization" and it could have existed on a quite small scale, of which the possibility can be studied even in the pitifully little data we possess on ancient agriculture.

The main factor is that small farming is always and everywhere a very risky proposition. It is enormously dependent on climatic features and especially the unforeseeably variable quantity and dating of the rain. It depends also on natural catastrophes like drouth, earthquake, cyclone (and war too) which are in a general way foreseeable. A further factor which cannot be overlooked is the sometimes brusquely and critically varying health of the small owner and the number and well-being of his children and other unpaid collaborators.

All these miseries menacing the small farmer are luridly portrayed in exegetical discusions of the debt-slavery which threatens him. What they never go on to inquire is to what extent these variables can be harnessed and coped with by efficient larger-scale management.

Distribution of ownership on several levels, not necessarily latifundism but some kind of cooperativism, first of all can divide and share the losses due to disaster. Secondly, it can make available land-plots in various climatic conditions, so that while one is suffering another may be sound. Thirdly, it can rotate crops and fallow, and for this can summon needed workmen from other areas where they are being less effective. Fourthly, it can reduce the number of those condemned to "debt-slavery" by selecting among them some of the more competent manager-types, and granting them

---

[11] Hans BARDTKE, "Die Latifundien in Juda während der zweiten Hälfte des achten Jahrhunderts v. Chr. (Jes 5,8-10)", *Hommage à A. DUPONT-SOMMER* (Paris 1971, A. Maisonneuve) 235-254.

an ever-increased level of authority.

If thus ultimately the "owners" of small fields become progressively just like tenants or "peons", and diminish or lose that proud sense of "independent ownership" handed down "from generation to generation", this would doubtless upon reflection be seen as less important than the insurance or guarantee that their daily bread is not dependent upon quirks of chance and weather, but will be equalized by sharing with similar small farmers.

Experts will doubtless see at once that any real ownership or "voice" left to the small less-competent owner would be subject to the vagaries of democracy, so that to continue functioning successfully it would be ever more subject to a kind of government "protection". At any rate we are dealing here with a long-ago choice among very simple alternatives: inalienable family ownership versus latifundism, or some kind of tenancy against the debt-threatening uncertainties of small farming.

Under the name latifundia our book dealt chiefly with the ancient Near East sources in which Eichrodt saw latifundism as "imposing itself almost with the necessity of nature"[12]. But we also noted the strictures of Isa 5,8 against "laying field to field"; Mi 2,2 "those who desire and seize fields, and oppress a yeoman of his heritage": Amos 5,11; 8,5 alluding to sharecropping on large landholdings.

Since then we have an example of the term latifundia to describe the contents of a book said to be the first great breakthrough in the history of exegesis toward utilizing not merely the Hebrew language and text but also the whole rabbinical context and its religious dimension. Cunaeus as professor of Latin and jurisprudence from 1615 in Leiden specialized in Josephus Flavius and especially Maimonides, and had contacts with Menasseh ben Israel and with Joseph Scaliger, Hugo Grotius, John Selden and other Christian Hebraists. Ziskind surveys his 1617 *De republica Hebraeorum* chiefly to find in the Jubilee "the perfect society ordained by God". But his comments on latifundia are mostly from Aristotle via Josephus or Maimonides.

Ziskind touches upon a subject which should have been examined more carefully by all of us who have had to deal with the question of whether the Jubilee was ever observed, as an aspect of whether it was a real law or just

---

[12] Walther EICHRODT, *OT Theology* (German [3]1933. 1,39) and his "Religionsgeschichte Israels" in F. KERN & F. VALJAVEC, ed., *Historia mundi* (Bern 1953) 2,385; R. NORTH, *Sociology of the Biblical Jubilee* 1954, p. 46 & 201; on Isa Mi Am there p.39.

a homily: namely, can there be a real obligation without a sanction for non-observance ? Cunaeus (or Maimonides) seems to hold that this is a necessity for human laws but not for divine, though "if the Jubilees were counted, why were they not observed ?". Nevertheless Ziskind denies, against Neufeld and me, that the Jubilee law could have been considered obligatory for at least one single time[13].

5. *Conclusions*

"The Land belongs to YHWH", despite recent claims either that it is the *people* who are his *naḥalâ*; or that God is dispossessing the Canaanite owners in favor of Israel. It has been generally assumed that what is called "God's ownership" means really "inalienable entailment of all lands in the same (extended) family to which they were assigned at the first settlement" though this formula is now seen to involve a certain intermingling of myth.

At any rate the overwhelming Jubilee concern for the restoration of the property of the defaulting small farmer (even if after 50 years or if he personally is dead or gone) is really a device for land-inalienability within the family: a two-edged sword regarding latifundism, insofar as some families may have few heirs and in others a rich Go'el can buy up many brothers' share.

It must thus not be considered obvious that the Jubilee solution for the divine ownership will be always and everywhere the most just and appropriate solution. Five others are distinguished purely theoretically within other books of the Bible itself, or by invoking an obscure "sociology of knowledge".

A King's right to distribute land or cancel debts is invoked surprisingly seldom in the Mid-East absolute monarchies, and then generally as a once-for-all event. Even David conceded that his predecessor's own property belonged to his heirs rather than to the new king.

A certain consideration is merited by a modern view that "God's land" should belong to those who can administer it most efficiently and for the greatest benefit of all, even if through a power obtained by complicated procedures hard to examine under the microscope of ethics.

But we should not too readily abandon the Jubilee-chapter favor for the small independent farmer. Though his work can scarcely be efficient enough

---

[13] Jonathan R. ZISKIND, "Petrus CUNAEUS on Theocracy, Jubilee, and the Latifundia", *JQR* 68 (Apr. 1978; 235-253) p. 242; 251.

to fit modern equipment and economics, we can detect in the very struggle against ever-threatening debt a hint that the small farmer might have more to gain from cooperation in local groups than from an "independence" which often really benefits his remote family more than himself.

Administration of such groups too would remain a problem: the more competent will tend to rise to the top, leaving the others to feel they are no more than serfs: unless they demand a kind of democratic voice in the procedures; but that too might tend to be counter-productive or lead to a disquieting government protectionism.

iv

Repurchase

The most immediate among the regulations consequent upon the Jubilee in Lev 25,14 is the limitation of sale of the land as a virtual rental up to the next Jubilee date. After brief mention of this, verse 25 goes on to an alternative for the Jubilee execution, the right of repurchase before that date. This repurchase (*gᵉ'ullâ*) has generally been called "Land-Redemption", and its next-of-kin purchaser (*gô'ēl*) the "Land-Redeemer".

1. Redeemer/Redemption: rather "Land Repurchase Rights"

We used that term "Redeemer" in our book, but we have tended to avoid it because of the strongly religious implications it has come to acquire. In part these involve a hint of fault or guilt from which the owner has to be "redeemed", and which is in principle not the case here[1].

More importantly, "Our Redeemer" has come to be a name for (Jesus or) God, and *gô'ēl* is used exclusively for God in Second-Isaiah[2]. That divine nuance is not entirely lacking in Lev 25, because it is ultimately as "Owner of All Land" that God, by the Jubilee, "repurchases" the land of its former

---

[1] Jeremiah UNTERMAN, *From Repentance to Redemption*: JSOT supp. 54. Sheffield 1987.
–- Johann J. STAMM, *Erlösen und Vergeben im Alten Testament* (Bern 1940), p. 142.

[2] Christopher R. NORTH [wrongly attributed to R(obert) North by Hartley's p. 416], "The Redeeming God", *Interpretation* 2 (1948) 3-16; p. 5 on *gô'ēl*. -- Richard J. SKLBA, "The Redeemer of Israel", *CBQ* 34 (1972; 1-38), citing on p.13 David DAUBE, *The Exodus Pattern in the Bible* (London 1961, Faber & Faber). -- Carroll STUHLMUELLER, *Creative Redemption in Deutero-Isaiah*: Analecta Biblica 42 (Rome 1970, Pontifical Biblical Institute); Samuele BACCHIOCCHI, "Sabbatical Typologies of Messianic Redemption", *JStJud* 17 (1986) 153-176; p 170, The Sabbath Years and Redemption.

owner, to guarantee that it will remain as "family possession", *'aḥuzzâ*.

As an aspect of a *gô'ēl*'s land-repurchase rights it is made explicit in Lev 25,23 that no sale of property can ever be "definitive, *endgültig*", the rare Hebrew and Ugaritic (but not Akkadian) term *šᵉmitut/šamātu*, meaning somewhat more than "forever"[3].

"In sociological contexts, redemption generally refers to the rescue of an individual from a difficult obligation by means of a monetary payment", chiefly the situation of an unpayable debt threatening or resulting in loss of ownership of farmland or house, with consequent tenancy or slavery; but applied also to levirate and blood-ransom (or *pādah*-ransom, or to the cultic "ransom" of the firstborn). "The *gô'el* was always the nearest adult male relative [apparently not counting the father], responsible for the economic well-being of his kin, inasmuch as the latter lacked sufficient means to redeem his own property"[4].

2. Repurchase in view of "Homecoming"

"The Go'el in Ancient Israel" is treated by Hubbard largely as a spicy paraphrase of Leviticus, dwelling with special complacency on the less-plausible aspects of the text, with no origins-tracing or explanation offered to render them more plausible. As for verse 26, it is admittedly unlikely that the ex-owner himself will ever scrape together enough for the repurchase, even by the rare possibilities suggested.

Even more strange is admitted to be verse 23, where YHWH's ownership of the land reduces the status of the human owner not only to that of a mere tenant but to that of a *foreign* tenant (*gēr*). What verse 24 aims to prevent is luridly described as "the rich [buyers] would bankroll their mortgages and increase their land holdings ... reap a handsome profit to be turned into other purchases, perhaps of more land ... a few wealthy land barons"[5].

Perhaps one cannot help wondering if these horrifying imaginings might not in some cases apply even to the Go'el, since it is common enough that

---

[3] Oswald LORETZ, "Ugaritisches ṣamātu und hebräisches ṣm(y)tt", *Biblische Zeitschrift* 6 (1962) 269-279, with evaluation of the dozen alternatives proposed since the publication of this Ugaritic term by J. NOUGAYROL in 1955.

[4] Jeremiah UNTERMAN, "Redemption (OT)", *Anchor Bible Dictionary* 5 (New York 1992, Doubleday) p. 650-654.

[5] Robert L. HUBBARD, Jr., "The Go'el in Ancient Israel; Theological Reflections on an Israelite Institution", *Bulletin for Biblical Research* 1 (1991, 1-19) 9 & 11. Relevance of the rendition "Redeemer" to both Judaism and Christianity is noted p. 72 (as DAUBE ftn 8,p.59).

in one family one of the brothers may become quite rich while several of the others are at the verge of bankruptcy. But no matter, just so the property remains inalienably in the family!

And in fact the final verses 47-55 envision the poor individual who is left penniless, as we shall treat in chapter 6 on "Debt". Hubbard rightly sees the Go'el as having an obligation here also: failing which, God himself as "the Great Kinsman" will release the "slave" by the Jubilee.

No matter if it is fifty long years away (and if irremediable bankrupts are usually past their twenties or even their thirties), there is always hope: the Jubilee amounts to "an institutional Exodus in Israel ... each instance of redemption amounts to a fresh moment of liberation, a miniature Exodus ... In the Jubilee the dominant note is their *home-coming*".

In Wright's view, the *g^e'ullâ* is intended mainly for the person, and may take place at any time; but the Jubilee only after 50 years aims to benefit mainly the "extended family", *bêt-abôt*[6]. Barton goes so far as to say, "There is nothing to suggest that *individuals* were regarded as holding their land on loan from God. What was central was the idea of *ancestral* land, .. (in a rather legendary way) as having been assigned by lot to each family at the time when the land was first settled"[7].

Daube devotes a part of one of his studies in biblical law to the institution of *g^e'ullâ*, and sees in Psalm 72,4 (the king shall save the children of the poor) a rather remote hint that if no close relative or other *gô'el* is available, the State has the obligation of performing this office of liberation for the disfranchised debtor[8].

3. Does the Gô'el keep for himself the land he repurchases?

Also rather negative on the inconsistencies in the overall structure of the Jubilee chapter is this statement with which an older article of Horst begins. "The Old Testament has no interest in giving us a complete and orderly

---

[6] Christopher J.H. WRIGHT, "Jubilee, Year of", *Anchor Bible Dictionary* 3 (1992) 1027.

[7] John BARTON, *Ethics and the OT* (London 1998, SCM) p. 54.

[8] David DAUBE, *Studies in Biblical Law* (Cambridge 1947, Univ.; 39-62) p. 45. -- Henry McKEATING, "Vengeance is Mine [Rom 12.19]: a Study of the Pursuit of Vengeance in the Old Testament", *Expository Times* 74 (1962-3; 239-245) p. 244 mentions the *gô'el* only in obscure relation to talion; his "The Development of the Law of Homicide in Ancient Israel", *VT* 25 (1974) 45-68 tries to show how D and P whittled away at making more humane the earlier clan-law system.

survey of the relation among Israelite laws, any more than it aims to clarify the historical development of Israel in the course of its political, cultural, and religious life"[9].

He thus prudently dispenses himself from falling into the vortex of dating and inconsistency-solving which perforce occupy most books of this kind, mine included. He contents himself with concluding that $d^e r \hat{o} r$ and $g^e' u l l \hat{a}$ on free land in God's service is the religious ideal of this social program.

"One aspect of this confusion is .. whether the 'redeemer', having bought the property, restored it to the impoverished brother (Noth, *Lev* p.189; Leggett) or kept it for himself (Pedersen, Daube, McKane). ... But 'consistency' here may be an unnecessary demand ... actual practice had [varying] aims and customs. ... Neufeld (*RSO* p.76) and North (1954 p.165f) are noncommittal on this question."[10]

Milgrom is not noncommittal. He begins with a "postulate" which in fact seems to be a wholly new alternative introduced into the discussion: "the *gô'el* retains the land he has redeemed and only in the Jubilee returns it to its original owner", and this is claimed to solve also a crux of Lev 25,33 about the jubilee return of a house repurchased from a Levite[11].

---

[9] Friedrich HORST, "Das Eigentum nach dem Alten Testament" [< *Das Eigentum als Problem evangelischer Sozialethik* (Essen 1949, Heft 2 p. 87-102] in his *Gottes Recht, Ges.Stud.* ed. Hans W. WOLFF: Theologische Bücherei 12 (München 1961, Kaiser) 203-221.

[10] Christopher J.H. WRIGHT, *God's People in God's Land: Family, Land, and Property in the Old Testament* (Grand Rapids/Exeter 1990, Eerdmans/Paternoster) 120. But I (now) share his surprise that the *father* is nowhere considered with or before the brother among next-of-kin *gô'ēl* candidates. -- Donald A. LEGGETT, *The Levirate and Goel Institutions in the Old Testament, with Special Attention to the Book of Ruth* (diss. Amsterdam 1974; Cherry Hill NJ 1974, Mack) p. 95, citing R.K. SIKKEMA, *De lening in het Oude Testament* ('s Gravenhage 1957) p. 11. -- J. PEDERSEN, *Israel, its Life and Culture* (London 1926, p. 84: on which Leggett cites NORTH p.186); Pedersen holds that the repurchased property was acquired by the god (for the family); so also David DAUBE, *The New Testament and Rabbinic Judaism* (1956, p. 272) and W. McKANE, 1962 W., "Ruth and Boaz", *Glasgow Univ. Oriental Soc. Transactions* 19 (1962) 35.

[11] Jacob MILGROM, "The Land Redeemer and the Jubilee", Fest. D.N. FREEDMAN, *Fortunate the Eyes that See*, ed. A. BECK, *al.* (Grand Rapids 1995, Eerdmans), p. 66-69. His p. 69 also attributes to Leviticus 25,40.53 the "revolutionary innovation" of completely eliminating the term "slave" used for an Israelite in Ex 21,1-11 and Deut 15,12-18.

4. Origin and early stages of gô'el

Johnson deals chiefly with the etymology of $gō'ēl$, which in the light of blood-avenger (Jg 9,5) and levirate (Ruth), he sees to mean "(clan life and property) protector" but with a nuance of the homonym which he takes to mean "cover" (like insurance) from an original sense "defile"[12].

An early stage of landholding belonging to the "family as such" has been claimed to be reflected in Lev 25,10 though denied by the Lev 25 Redactor. Kippenberg in fact cites for $gô'el$ and related terms various Lev 25 passages without adequately indicating how controversial their meaning is[13].

The "levirate" obligation to have a son by his brother's widow (Deut 25,5), by comparison with Ruth 3,13, may be seen to have had an intention similar to that of the $g^e'ullâ$: permanence of property within the family. A highly relevant example of $g^e'ullâ$ is given in Jer 32. While in prison in relation to a Babylonian siege of King Zedekiah, Jeremiah as $gô'el$ and nearest relative (verse 7) buys from his cousin Hanamel a field in Anathoth. Though this event here forms part of an "acted-out prophecy" for God's decree in verse 15, "Houses and fields and vineyards shall again be bought in this land", still the details and recording of the transaction shed light on what the practice of $g^e'ullâ$ would have been like[14].

Perhaps as a later development may be considered the eschatological senses of the repurchase laws, which we examine in ch. 8 in relation to Isa 61 and Lk 4. But Unterman ends his AnchorBD treatment of "Redemption" with a section which he calls "Conceptual Meaning: The Eschatological Age of Redemption" in which he cites not Lev 25 but Lev 26,40. His preceding section, "The God-Israel Relationship" (which we broached in footnotes 1 and 4 above), is called the "metaphorical meaning" of $g^e'ullâ$-redemption as release from (Egypt) exile, not really mirrored in Lev 25.

---

[12] Aubrey R. JOHNSON., "The Primary Meaning of Root $\sqrt{gō'ēl}$", *Copenhagen 1953 Congress Volume*: VT supp. 1 (1953) 67-77.

[13] H.G. KIPPENBERG, *Religion und Klassenbildung im antiken Judäa. Eine religionssoziologische Studie zum Verhältnis von Tradition und Entwicklung*: SUNT 14 (Göttingen 1978, Vandenhoeck & Ruprecht) p. 25; 22; cited by MEINHOLD p.259.

[14] Compare also Nahum SARNA, "Zedekiah's Emancipation of Slaves and the Sabbatical Year, Jer 34,12-16", in Fest. C. GORDON, *Orient and Occident*, ed. H. HOFFNER: AOAT 22 (Kevelaer/Neukirchen 1973) 143-9.

5. Conclusions

The g^e*'ullâ* is the right and obligation of repurchase (often called redemption) of a defaulting debtor's property by his next of kin *gô'el*, immediately or at any time up to the effecting of this by the Jubilee. The recovering of his land by the dispossessed debtor is equivalent to his homecoming, even if he is still living on that plot of land as a tenant-serf. If he is no longer alive, the land remains (presumably via the *gô'el*) property of his family. Such an occurrence, sooner or later, is ultimately presented as the more important aspect of the decree.

The g^e*'ullâ* is thus importantly related to the levirate obligation to have childen by one's brother's widow in order to keep property within the extended family. This is basically also the background of the Book of Ruth.

It is not made clear (or considered important) whether the *gô'el* keeps title to the land for himself or restores it to his relative; nor whether in any case the defaulting debtor continues as a tenant, though this rather seems to be the case in the modes of expression in the later parts of the chapter (apart from "homecoming").

The g^e*'ullâ* has further an important religious or mystical aspect in Judaism and Christianity, in relation to "God our Redeemer" and our eschatological hope of salvation.

V

Loans

This chapter is really about the loans on which there is briefly stated a prohibition of "interest"; but its real interest is something quite different. "Usury" as Stein indicates has medieval implications. He gives the only examples of an actual interest-rate in loans between Jews, a whopping 60% declared to be not unusual among others at Elephantine[1].

1. *Sitz im Leben of Leviticus 25,35-38*

"The examination of the jubilee law shows that it is an editorial combination of some well-known subjects -- fallow year, levitical cities, redemption, slavery, and loans -- to which a new interpretation was given", says Yairah Amit quite tenably, adding that the time of composition of the jubilee at the end of all this legislation supports her view that H (Holiness Code Lev 17-26) is as late as P (Pentateuch Priestly source) or later[2].

---

[1] S. STEIN, "The Laws on Interest in the Old Testament", *JTS NS* 4 (1953; 161-170) p. 160; 169 from COWLEY-Elephantine 10 & 11. -- Benjamin NELSON, *The Idea of Usury* [*Usura e cristianesimo, per una storia dell'etica moderna*, tr. S. MORAVIA, Firenze 1967, Sansoni].

[2] Yairah AMIT, "The Jubilee Law -- an Attempt at Instituting Social Justice", in Henning REVENTLOW and Yair HOFFMAN, ed., *Justice and Righteousness; Biblical Themes and their Influence* (Bochum 1990): JSOT supp. 137 (Sheffield 1992; 47-59) 55. On p. 54 she rejects this "solution" cited from my 1954 work without page: "Each land-sale had its own jubilee and we cannot speak of an application of the law to all the lands of the state". Like most commentators on the extremely controverted and variously-membered Jubilee-law formulation, I evaded making too point-blank statements as to what the law meant "exactly and nothing else". Her citation may apply to the particular sub-problem I am dealing with on my p. 189; but most authors cite me more acceptably as saying on p. 209 that the jubilee was intended as a law, practicable and probably practiced the first time, after 50 years, but after that it proved unworkable but was retained as an ideal. She cites also as unsupportive of her own

Whether this is the case or not will depend largely on whether we can regard H as more entirely creative (at some stage after the P-traditions had been rather fully formulated) while P(-Redactor) itself tends recently to be seen as the very last compilational stage. In either case we may still regard the actual jubilee as the last notable insertion into Lev 25, which then served to organize all the rest.

Among the earliest fragments available to the compiler is generally included the one relating to the prohibition of taking interest on loans. This is a very brief but forceful passage, Lev 25,35-38; and in fact verse 37 really carries the whole weight, according to Elliger: "in chiastic *parallelismus membrorum*, even metrically structured: an originally poetic form ...evidently an ancient dictum in verse"[3].

Except for its outdatedness, Hejcl's *Zinsverbot* with its stress on "ethnological jurisprudence" would have furnished material for an interesting dialogue with Elliger. Hejcl agrees that the most ancient ethical norms are often in proverbial form, though denying this as a criterion that the antecedents of Lev 25,37 in Ex 22,24 are older then those of Deut 23.20, to which Lev 25,36 gives "a juristic explanation and expansion". But he finally agrees that the humane aspects of the prohibition of interest mark it as very ancient, "a Semitic *Urgesetz* written in the hearts of the *Ursemiten*"[4].

Lev 25,36 uses the two terms for (usurious) interest: *nešek* and *tarbît* (*marbît* for "food", verse 37). In Ex 22,24 occurs *nešek*, but in parallel with a participial *nôšeh*. "Hejcl (p. 68) excludes the possibility that ancient Israel could have already advanced to such an extent as to have a *nôseh* as 'professional moneylender' [< Akkadian *râšû*] here simultaneously a manifestation of the strong aversion to the Canaanite laws and customs"[5].

In Deut 23,20 we have only *nešek*, but rhetorically repeated three times:

---

position Sara JAPHET, "Laws concerning Freeing the Slaves and the Relationship between Collections of Laws in the Torah", in Fest. S.E. LOEWENSTAMM, *Studies in the Bible and the Ancient Near East* p.231-250 (1978, Hebrew; there p. 183-205, I.L. SEELIGMANN, "Lending, Pledge and Interest in Biblical Law and Hebrew Thought).

[3] K. ELLIGER, *Leviticus* 1966, p.340.

[4]   Johann HEJCL, *Das alttestamentliche Zinsverbot im Lichte der ethnologischen Jurisprudenz sowie des altorientalischen Zinswesens*: Biblische Studien 12,1 (Freiburg 1906, Herder), p 67; 78; 84.

[5] Edward NEUFELD, "The Prohibitions against Loans at Interest in Ancient Hebrew Laws", *HUCA* 26 (1955; 355-412) p.375, concerned only with how *early* commercial loans at interest became permitted in Israel, agreeing in principle with Hejcl. On *nešek/tarbît* Neufeld p.255.

no *nešek* (on a loan) of money, no *nešek* of food, no *nešek* of anything on which one gives interest. Neufeld (p.358) makes much of the fact that unlike Ex 22,24, poverty has nothing to do with it; *nešek* is forbidden on loans to *anyone* [at that stage of commercial development!]. This is followed in Deut 23,21 by an explicit permission to charge interest on loans to foreigners (p.53n7; possible justification of this will be noted (Hejcl also p. 53).

2. Force of the obligation of "keeping a fellow-Israelite alive"

We have asserted that in Lev 25,35-38 there is no real concern for either loans or interest to be paid on them. The stress is chiefly on the positive obligation of "keeping *alive with you* (saving from inability to work his farm) a brother ... out of respect for the God who had equally saved both out of Egypt". We venture even to say that "loan" is never explicit in verse 35, and where implicit in verses 36 and 37, it would be rather a *gô'el*-type loan.

Yet it is not presented as exactly a gift either. It may in fact be such, logically. But in most languages "gift" has rather loftier nuances, and in cases of desperation one would even today perhaps rather euphemistically speak of a "loan".

What we have is ancient (Ex Deut) traditions against profiting by loans, traditions now confronted with a man's or whole family's livelihood at stake. A crisis has arisen to which neither a gift nor properly speaking a loan is the prescribed reaction, but "keeping your brother alive with you". Even if you give him enough food for his family today, there is no likelihood that tomorrow he will be able to pay you back at all, with or without interest.

Indeed, more than likely tomorrow he will still be without anything to eat! But starvation is not really the issue, as if Lev 25,35 could be paraphrased "if his situation is so desperate, you are really obliged to invite him to share your family meals, or their leftovers, for a few days or long enough so that he can make some other arrangement". The real sense of "keep him alive with you" in this context is "keep him able to own and work his farm".

The situation is not really that of a small loan chiefly of food (mentioned in the traditions of Deut 23,20 on which the prohibition seems to be based) or perhaps of coppers to procure it (as Ex 22,24). The question of a loan big enough for long-range solution is not raised. But in the option of a relative-*gô'el* who resolves the desperate farmer's situation by repurchase there would obviously be question of a big sum of money (but also of its recompense by keeping the farm -- at least within the family).

To understand the real significance of this "loan to keep alive" decree, we must try to project ourselves back into the cultural framework of the final compilation, yes -- but also of the far remote past from which it stemmed, as shown above.

In cities of today we are frequently accosted by beggars. There is no suitable term for what they are requesting; it would hardly be considered either a "gift" or a "loan"; an "alms" would fit, but that is slightly archaic or has religious nuances not always pertinent. Some of the beggars look so perfectly the part of the barely surviving absolutely destitute -- filthy rags, unkempt hair, unctuous whines -- that many passers-by are tempted to regard it as "putting on an act", and hurry on without giving anything.

Many others, however, in this as well as less picturesque cases give something for fear of failing in a grave duty. Others give to everyone indiscriminately, because "what you have done to the least of my brethren you have done also to me" (Mt 25,40). Some few have at the tip of their tongue the address of a nearby hospice or soup-kitchen or religious group offering what is needed precisely for the desperate.

Most people know that such institutions exist and perform a constant useful service in that city, but have no idea of the address of a suitable one. We all know, however, that such institutional services for the destitute did *not* exist in biblical times, and that the sufferer's only hope lay in a charitable "loan" from a neighbor. The question of "interest" or payment for such a loan would scarcely even arise.

Thus even the mention of *nešek* or *tarbît* here seems inopportune, perhaps a self-evident restriction inserted by a compiler from a later and more commercial age. At any rate, there is obviously all the difference in the world between a "loan" made for the very livelihood of oneself and one's family, and a prosperous profitable borrowing.

We must note finally that even the Deut 23,20 parallel prohibition of interest on a loan to a poor Israelite, though from the Kings era and thus despite Hejcl doubtless much later than the "poetic-proverbial" original form explained above by Elliger, adds unblushingly, "You may demand interest from a foreigner, but not from your countryman". The implication may well be, not merely that the foreigner has somewhat less a claim on "disinterested" charity, but rather "because such cases were strictly business deals"[6].

---

[6] Louis F. HARTMAN, tr. ed. A. VAN DEN BORN (*Bijbels Woordenboek* [2]1957), "Loans", *Encyclopedic Dictionary of the Bible* (New York 1963, McGraw-Hill), p. 1361, citing J. HEJCL, *Das alttestamentliche Zinsverbot* 1906 (ftn. 4 above).

"The lending of silver, chattel, or produce may not give occasion to charging interest, unless the borrower is a non-Israelite [Deut 15,3; 23,21][7]". To understand properly such discrimination, it is necessary to premise a general survey of loans at interest among Israel's neighbors.

3. Loans at interest in the Ancient Near East background

Hejcl's "ethnographic jurisprudence" survey, though missing the many discoveries and new evaluations of the entire past century (several of which are dealt with on p. 66 below), can serve as an orderly starting-point. His *Zinsverbot* treats Mesopotamian money-use and loans p.22-56 and Egypt p.18-21. He does not give a similar preliminary on Canaanites or the Phoenicians of nearby Tyre, except when on p. 69 and 76 he stresses their importance for Israel's commercial needs, and the disadvantage it would be for Israel, while having to pay interest on loans *from* neighboring peoples, not to be able to charge interest on loans *to* them.

Some few more recent studies may be mentioned here. One is pre-Hammurabi[8]. Another is on the late-Babylonian *hubutt(at)um* described as "interest-free but not necessarily profit-free"[9].

A research by Maloney concludes that loans on interest were permitted throughout the Near East except in Israel, and that the rate was around 20% to 25%. Obviously even this rate would be considered rather high, and consequently its exclusion from Israel was normal. He does not consider further the case of Israel, or whether and at what time loans at a lower rate of interest were legitimate[10].

Within the Bible, the problem of usury must doubtless be linked to neighboring usage, or to the Kings era when it first became prominent[11]. Expositors distinguish business-enterprise loans, on which even high rates of

---

[7] G.A. BARROIS, "Debt, debtor", *Interpreter's Dictionary of the Bible* 1 (1962) 309 -- Christiana VAN HOUTEN, *The Alien in Israelite Law*: JSOT.S 107. Sheffield 1991.

[8] Émile SZLECHTER, "Le prêt dans l'Ancient Testament et dans les Codes mésopotamiens d'avant Hammourabi", *RHPR* 35 (1995) 16-25.

[9] Lawrence SHIFF, "Neo-Babylonian 'Interest-Free' Promissory Notes". *Journal of Cuneiform Studies* 40 (1988) 187-194, citing E. BILGIÇ 1947.

[10] Robert P. MALONEY, "Usury and Restrictions on Interest-Taking in the Ancient Near East", *CBQ* 56 (1974) 1-20.

[11] Erhard S. GERSTENBERGER, *Leviticus*: ATDeutsch 6 (1993) 355; A. ALT, "Der Anteil des Königtums an der sozialen Entwicklung in den Reichen Israel und Juda" [< Fest. J. LEIPOLDT 1955] in his *Kleine Schriften* 3 (1959) 348-372.

interest could be allowed, from loans made to a needy neighbor in trouble.

From a slightly postbiblical period at Elephantine we have noted in ftn.1 above a thriving business in moneylending, in which Jews even among themselves took part, and in which the recorded interest-rates were far higher than 25%; nearer to 60% on the whole.

"Inventive means were found in Judaism after the biblical period: Hillel's *prosbul* [Sheb 10,3-6; Git 36a ...]; Hillel allows the debts to be entrusted by the creditor to a court, which could collect the debts for him, [not to evade Torah but in view of the altered economy and] changes in the market value of commodities"[12].

4. Debated biblical legitimacy of commercial loans at interest

As we have observed, the legitimacy of charging interest on a loan to a non-Israelite carries with it a slight hint that such loans were more likely to be requested for profitable business purposes than for a desperate vital need.

Nowadays "personal" loans are generally to buy a house or a car, with built-in interest rates fixed in the price by the seller; or as a (second) mortgage to keep up the payments. In the Western world at least we scarcely consider a loan as a way of just keeping alive from one day to the next. But that was obviously the concern of the biblical laws against taking interest.

These laws occur in the same three areas as other poor-relief measures eventually put in relation to the Jubilee. Ex 22,24 says "If thou lendest *kesep* to my people [G to your brother] to the poor with thee, thou shalt not be to him as a moneylender [*nôšeh*, verb roughly synonym of *nôše'*, milder than *nešek* "bite"], ye shall [G S thou shalt] not lay upon him interest (*nešek*)". But a cloak (*śimlâ* and metathesis *śalmâ* both used in verse 25-26) may be taken as a pledge (*ḥebel*) for the daylight hours only.

In this verse only *kesep* is lent; in Deut 23,22 "*kesep*, food, or anything else"; in Lev 25,36 "*kesep* or food" and in verse 37 the prohibited interest on *kesep* is *nešek* but on food is *marbît*. In these cases *kesep* is usually rendered "money, a medium of exchange probably copper or silver" as already in the days of Abraham, Gen 20,16.

---

[12] Bruce CHILTON, "Debts", *Anchor Bible Dictionary* 2 (1992) 114, citing Jacob NEUSNER, *School, Court, Public Administration; Judaism and its Institutions in Talmudic Babylonia*: Brown Judaic Studies 83 (Atlanta 1987, Scholars) p. 248-256. As virtually in *IDB*, there is no article in *AnchorBD* on Interest except Greco-Roman period and a reference to Debt(s), which (unlike our ch.6 on Debt-"slavery") treats mostly post-OT loans.

But if we endeavor to think ourselves back into the earliest periods in which the problem of interest on moneylending came to the fore, it is probably overhasty to think of really silver being involved (though that is what *kesep* literally means) -- even apart from the ancient millennium-long procedures of weighing (*šeqel*) to be sure of the exact value, until coinage was invented only after 600 in the Persian era[13].

"We are dealing here with a community which is familiar with standardized measures of silver ... and in which loans at interest become an important factor" says Neufeld at the very outset of his study (ftn.5 above). This would be easy to accept in the rather common view that the Jubilee was compiled in the Persian era. Even in copying traditions of Exodus or Deuteronomy the compiler may have inserted references to money as it was known to him. Neufeld adds however that the standardized silver "served as a kind of currency and already takes the place of cattle and other goods" -- which may leave us wondering whether he refers to Mosaic or Kings era.

At any rate, insofar as the final form of the Jubilee chapter and indeed of the whole Pentateuch is more generally considered to have been dated in the Persian era, it is not surprising that the compiler should casually use the term "money" in passing on fragments from earlier periods. But since we are here investigating precisely the function of a loan for a debtor's very livelihood, as distinct from a commercial operation or even from the big sums which are implied in the land-sale or repurchase norms of the Jubilee chapter, we ought to pose the question of whether a loan in food or seed-grain would be more opportune than silver or even copper.

In fact Lev 25,37 speaks of a loan of "money *or food*", while Deut 23,20 goes even farther and says "money, food, or anything else". For this reason the Deuteronomic form is held by Gamoran to be more progressive and recent, and even to involve *four* changes of Ex not in Lev[14]. But the

---

[13] H. HAMBURGER, "Money", *Interpreter's Dictionary of the Bible* 3 (1962) 423-435; G. MAYER, "*kesep*", *ThWAT* 4 (1982) 283-297 = TDOT 7 (tr. D. GREEN 1995) 270-282; John W. BETLYON (on money), *AnchorBD* 1 (1992) p. 1076-9 of "Coinage" p. 1076-1089.

[14] Hillel GAMORAN, "The Biblical Law against Loans on Interest", *JNES* 30 (1971; 127-134) p. 129; 133; "The Talmudic Law of Mortgages in View of the Prohibition against Lending on Interest", *HUCA* 52 (1981) 153-162; "Mortgages in Geonic Times in Light of the Law against Usury", *HUCA* 68 (1997) p.97-109, "Sura mortgages" apparently similar to Jubilee "sale". --See also Walter HOUSTON, "'You Shall Open your Hand to your Needy Brother'; Ideology and Moral Formation in Deut 15:1-18", in J.W. ROGERSON ed., *The Bible in Ethics*: JSOT supp. 207 (Sheffield 1995) 296-314 [Margaret DAVIES 315-343 NT slavery].

principal aim of his article seems to be to reject Neufeld's view that "'the law against lending on interest as stated in Exodus intended that the prohibition be limited to the poor alone. He suggests that commercial loans at interest were permissible.' This theory cannot be accepted"[15].

Both exegetes seem to draw their proof chiefly from the fact that in the whole Bible there is no statement whatever on commercial loans or on interest chargeable for them. This is indeed a significantly relevant fact; but it is a two-edged sword. Gamoran speaks of the "blanket prohibition against interest in Deuteronomy, which does not mention the poor", yet he admits that the Deuteronomic version was written for the poor and for their protection.

Ultimately as the old joke has it, he seems to be saying "everything is forbidden which is not explicitly permitted" and Neufeld "everything is permitted which is not explicitly forbidden". This latter principle seems to be legally more sound. Or rather what points in Neufeld's favor is that in interpreting any somewhat dubious law we should take into account the *Sitz im Leben*, the real-life vital situation in which the law is imbedded. There is no indication that the biblical laws show any concern whatever for commercial loans, whether with or without interest.

Neufeld's *HUCA* 1955 has a section entitled "Commercial Standards and Temple Loans in Israel" (p. 376), in which he maintains that especially in the thriving commercial activity under Solomon, loans from the Temple were quite an ordinary thing, though totally unmentioned in the Pentateuch, and "may possibly" even have charged interest.

To this he adds (p. 381) "The Talmud, however, offers strong evidence to the effect that Temple loans at interest were transacted in ancient Israel. According to a B⁰rayta [Baba Meṣî'a 57b] the Tannaim held that the Temple transactions were not subject to the laws of usury [and their discussions show that] in a circuitous manner the Temple actually received interest on loans".

With this undoubtedly interesting citation, Neufeld perhaps by "proving too much" harms his own case for the legitimacy of commercial loans in biblical times. He admits the disapproval of the Amoraim for these Tannaitic discussions, and their general vagueness. But the very fact which he most stresses, namely that in biblical times commercial loans at interest were

---

[15] GAMORAN *JNES* 30 (1971), p. 131, citing Edward NEUFELD, "The Prohibition against Loans at Interest in Ancient Hebrew Laws", *HUCA* 26 (1955) 398; "The Rate of Interest and the Text of Nehemiah 5:11 [12%]", *JQR* 44 (1953) 194-204.

legitimate, is to some extent disproved by the observation that Temple-loans by dispensation were able to charge interest. Neufeld's case might have been stronger if he remained satisfied with his position that the known gradual economic development made loans at interest for commercial purposes likely, while nothing whatever is said about them in the prohibition of interest on "loans" to the desperately poor.

"The formulation of these laws against making loans at interest does not address the issue of loaning money at interest for a commercial enterprise. .. Neufeld may be correct in suggesting that these laws against interest may not cover all situations of lending money. Unfortunately, there is insufficient information to resolve this matter"[16].

Our concern here is not to take issue on Neufeld's side, but rather to stress with Gamoran that these biblical laws are wholly concerned with helping the desperately poor to preserve their livelihood. What the biblical formulations and the natural law itself really command is that in a desperate situation the neighbor must *give* as a "loan" what is needed. Softly in the background may be heard that "desperate" here really means "debts so burdening the small farmer that he is losing his property" -- and his family's.

5. *Conclusions*

The briefly-stated prohibition of "interest" or usury on loans to a fellow-Israelite in Lev 25,35-38 is treated here chiefly in view of the also-brief qualification "to keep him alive with you". The loans thus spoken of are thus in a situation of desperation and practically unrepayable, therefore really "alms" or "gifts" as a basic grave obligation of charity, rather than concerned with the "interest" (*nešek* and/or *tarbît*) which was known to be charged on some kinds of loans.

The parallel prohibition regarding poor Israelites in Deut 23,20 adds explicitly that to demand interest on a loan to foreigners is legitimate. This concession may imply that it was advantageous to Israel to have commercial or business dealings with the Phoenicians of Tyre or the Canaanites or other neighboring nations which charged interest on the loans they made to

---

[16] HARTLEY, *Leviticus*: p. 440. -- David J.A. CLINES, "Haggai's Temple: Constructed, Deconstructed and Reconstructed" [it was a bank: Rome 1991 SBL meeting], in *Second Temple Studies 2*, ed. T. ESKENAZI: JSOT supp. 175, Sheffield 1994, p. 60-87; J. BLENKINSOPP, "Temple and Society in Achaemenid Judah", in *Second Temple Studies 1*, ed. P. DAVIES: *JSOT* supp. 117, Sheffield 1991, p. 22-53: in Neh 12,13; 2 Mcb 3,5-18; Josephus War 6,282 & AntB14,110-3: "the Temple served as .. bank: private funds deposited".

Israelites. Reciprocity would seem to warrant that Israelites could charge interest on these foreigners in return; otherwise Israel would be left at an unfair disadvantage.

The wider extent of interest-charging in the influential neighboring empires or even in postbiblical Jewish practice is studied for purposes of comparison. It is noted that the *nešek* or *tarbit* "interest" prohibited on biblical loans is generally given in terms of *kesep,* "silver or money". This term may possibly have been inserted into more archaic texts at the presumed time of the final compilation of the Pentateuch, in the Persian era in which coinage had been invented and become normative.

But the historical background has commonly been taken to support the view that within Israel itself there was gradually developing, especially during and after the reign of Solomon, a flourishing commercial orientation quite different from the petty-agriculture focus with which most of the Jubilee chapter deals,

Hence there has arisen a controversy as to whether also in higher-level commercial dealings between Israelites themselves it had gradually become regarded as legitimate to charge a moderate interest. Since our only biblical references to the matter, even where plainly concerned with the desperation of "being kept alive", nevertheless formulate the prohibition of interest in universal terms without qualification, some maintain that biblical law excludes also any interest on commercial loans. Others nevertheless plausibly argue that "whatever is nowhere explicitly prohibited is licit" and refer to a rabbinical note that even loans made by the Temple (unmentioned in the Bible) could charge interest.

vi

Debt

This chapter is about what is generally called "Debt-Slavery". Some especially Jewish commentators insist that the term "slave" is never applied to an Israelite in the Bible. Certainly it would be unlikely that *'ebed* always means that, instead of sometimes "servant, hired man, worker (or even 'son' in Isa/NT)".

1. What is the real or normal meaning of "slave"?

Today our general understanding of the "literal" meaning of slave probably depends chiefly on the sad and deplorable experience of the cotton-raising areas before the U.S. civil war. These slaves were all black and had been sold first by power-holders in their own Africa, then after an unspeakably inhumane caged ocean-voyage sold again in public slave-markets to white buyers, who in some cases treated them with decency but are generally considered to have beaten them and punished them in other cruel ways to force them to long hours of back-breaking work.

Perhaps the second-most-important source of our common understanding of slavery derives from the Roman Empire's captives or prisoners of war. Leaving aside the utter savagery of galley-slaves, the slaves usually mentioned or shown in the movies were frequently or perhaps generally of roughly the same race or color as their captors, and often of a comparable level of culture and education. Thus though they too were often treated with cruelty depending on the kind of work they had been bought to perform, with a cultured master they were sometimes enviably treated as *paidagōgós* or *au pair* companion to his son, and often granted full freedom in the prime of life: at least such cases have most impressed us in the classic authors.

It must be recognized from the start that "slave" is never used in the Old Testament in either of these two senses. He is never a war-captive nor kidnaped from a foreign race. He is always "legitimately bought", as (apparently willing, or by his father's decision) resident alien in Lev 25,44; but only "bought out" as (Israelite) defaulting debtor in all the other occurrences with which this volume deals: thus not only should "(debt-) slavery" be replaced by simply "debt" as claimed above, but "slave" also should be translated (or at least understood as) "debtor-tenant"[1].

Nowhere in the parts of the Old Testament with which we are dealing is "slave" used for captive or kidnaped foreigner, even though pre-modern slave-owners were often very religious Christians, and in assiduously reading their Bible took for granted that the "slaves" it spoke of were just like theirs. Though this outlook may have helped them somewhat toward treating their slaves humanely, it nevertheless gave them a very warped view of the biblical "slaves" who were simply "debtors" and had to work off their indebtedness more or less as anyone today has to work to pay off debts.

This opens out to us at once another aspect of slavery, as the denial of freedom. Freedom gets a lot of lip-service today, and like enslavement is used in a wide gamut of senses varying from maximally literal to unashamedly metaphorical. We might risk accepting the far-from-original contention that freedom is in essence a correlative of order: the more freedom, the less orderliness; or, we want freedom for ourselves but not for others.

Consider briefly the position of the "slave" called such in the Bible in all the passages with which this volume has to deal, not only in Leviticus 25 but also in Exodus 21 and Deuteronomy 15. He is clearly a man who had been a property-owner but now is a tenant-farmer. But this does not make him any less "free".

He still has to get up early and work hard all day just as he did when the land was his own. But he is also just as free as he then was to make his own schedule, sleep late sometimes or maybe even take an unnoticed holiday. Of course if the new owner actually lives on that farm (and there is no indication of such in our sources), he could supervise a more rigid schedule.

In any case, the tenant has to deliver a suitable crop, and in due time: none of the cited biblical passages indicate how this "suitable" is determined,

---

[1] N.P. LEMCHE, "The Hebrew Slave. Comments on the Slave Law Ex. xxi 2-11", *VT* 25 (1975) 129-144, -- I.J. GELB, "Quantitative Evaluation on Slavery or Serfdom", *S.N. Kramer Anniversary Volume*: AOAT 25 (Kevelaer/Neukirchen 1976; 195-208) p. 201, Mid-East captives were not enslaved but resettled; J.P.M. VAN DER PLOEG, "Slavery in the Old Testamemt", *Uppsala 1971 Congress Volume*: VTS 22 (Leiden 1972, Brill) 73-87.

but we may be sure that the *pro tem* owner must recognize that it depends far more on the weather (and even on purely natural variations of health) than any factor such as how "freely" the tenant lined up his daily chores.

One exegete dealing with the "slavery" of debt remarked the common phrase that *everybody* is "slave" of his function. It is a grand thing to be the sole owner of your own little farm, no doubt (and that holds for the ancient and some areas of the modern world, though it is totally impractical where efficient farming requires cooperative and technical developments). But your ownership-title makes relatively little difference in how "free" you are in your actual daily living.

Nowadays almost every job-holder has to get up early, commute far distances, live in constant anxiety about living or improving his job (and "social reform" includes invariably greater job-availability). But even the wealthy and the powerful can often remain such only by rigid subservience to the maneuvers required by their type of power. On a bus abroad I once overheard a prosperous foreigner say, "Last year I had no car; but I'm not going to put up with that slavery any more!"

2. The "Hebrew 'ebed" as ḥabiru slave

It was formerly common to find a technical sense of slave in the Ex 21,2 combination *'ebed 'ibrî*, taking *'ibrî* "Hebrew; descendant of Eber Gen 8,16" as equivalent of *ḥabiru, 'aperu,* widely used in both cuneiform and Egyptian as a somewhat-ethnic term but more oriented toward a gypsy fringe life-style[2]. The real force of *ḥabiru* here remains ambiguous, says Shalom Paul in noting that the combination *ḥabiru*-slave is nowhere found in cuneiform[3].

Now a thorough study by Loretz insists that *ḥabiru* is never ethnic and *'ibrî* is always ethnic, never sociological. He correlates this view with his assurance that *'ibrî* occurs only in the *later* OT passages (Gen 39-43; Ex 1-11). Very ancient are admitted to be the narratives in 1 Sam 4-29, but eight

---

[2] H.L. ELLISON, "The Hebrew Slave; a Study in Early Israelite Society", *Evangelical Quarterly* 45 (1973; 30-35) p. 36, "'Hebrew slave' was a technical expression antedating Moses", citing Albrecht ALT [< "Die Ursprünge des israelitischen Rechts", *Verhandlungen der sächsischen Akademie ph/h* 86,1 (Leipzig 1934)] "The Origins of Israelite Law", Eng. by R. A. WILSON 1966 = Biblical Seminar 9 (Sheffield 1989, JSOT Press; pp. 79-132) p. 94.

[3] Shalom M. PAUL, *Studies in the Book of the Covenant in the Light of Cuneiform and Biblical Law*: VTS 18 (Leiden 1970, Brill) p. 45.

uses of *'ibrî* in them are held to be postexilic additions[4]. Occurrence in Ex 21,2-11 is held to presuppose the sabbath-idea and therefore to be later than the parallel Deut 15,12-18. Rejection of this view that no pre-ethnic nuance survives in *'ibrî* by Lemche is based largely on Jonah 2,9[5].

Weippert's more general survey gives a four-page table justifying the insistence that the Akkadian form should be *ḫapiru* as in Egyptian *'apiru,* and that their Amarna-period uprising included local kings and their followers rather than only local peasants against their cities and rulers as in the Mendenhall-style non-violent revolt[6].

We will not attempt to survey here the many other studies devoted even recently to the *ḫabiru*. But it is worth noting the original suggestion that the designation of intrusive Israelites as Hebrews became prominent chiefly while they were getting the upper hand over the highland Canaanites thanks to their unity under YHWH and their more advanced agricultural and economic techniques[7].

3. Weil and the "slave" as Pledge: "Live-Gage" for mort-gage

My greatest surprise upon going through the various authors of the past fifty years who mention my book as a source, is the little or no attention paid to my dependence on Weil's 1938 "Gage et cautionnement dans la Bible"[8].

---

[4] Oswald LORETZ, *Habiru-Hebräer. Eine sozio-linguistische Studie über die Herkunft des Gentiliziums 'ibrî vom Appellativum ḫabiru*: BZAW 160 (Berlin 1984) p. 117; 182; not supported by Nadiv NA'AMAN, "Habiru and Hebrews; the Transfer of a Social Term to the Literary Sphere", *JNES* 45 (1986) 271-258. See further Mary P. GRAY, "The *Habiru*-Hebrew Problem in the Light of the Source Material Available at Present", *HUCA* 29 (1958; 135-202); p. 183, *'ebed-'ibrî.*

[5] N.P. LEMCHE, "The Hebrew and the Seven Year Cycle", *Biblische Notizen* 25 (1984; 65-75) p. 68, citing his "'Hebrew' as a National Name for Israel", *Studia Theologica* 33 (1979; 1-23) p. 10.

[6] Manfred WEIPPERT, *The Settlement of the Israelite Tribes in Palestine; a Critical Survey of Recent Scholarly Debate* [< *Die Landnahme*, FRLANT 92, Göttingen 1967], tr. James D. MARTIN (London 1972, SCM) 74-79.

[7] P.A. MUNCH, "Die wirtschaftliche Grundlage des israelitischen Volksbewusstseins vor Saul. Ein Beitrag zur Vorgeschichte Israels", *ZDMG* 92 (1939; 217-253, p. 219, 239, 253 (apparently not mentioned in the ample treatment of *ḫabiru* p.205-213 in CHIRICHIGNO 1993 below, nor in his bibliography or index).

[8] Hermann M. WEIL, "Gage et cautionnement dans la Bible", *Archives d'Histoire du Droit Oriental* 2 (1938; 171-240) p. 188; 195; 236 [also "Exégèse de Jér 23,33-4 et de Job 14,28-33", *Revue de l'Histoire des Religions* 118 (1938) 201-208]; my *Sociology* 1954 p.181-4; GERSTENBERGER ATD Lev 348. -- Now B. KIENAST, "Bemerkungen zum altassyrischen

Gerstenberger even remarks casually that the rule for "repurchase" cannot imply *Pfand*, "pledge", *maššâ*. The lengthy 1989 doctorate of Chirichigno however deals in detail with my use of Weil[9].

Max Weber had considered the possibility that what the jubilee law aims at is *antichrēsis*, a form of mortgage in which the creditor has the usufruct as well as the custody and *Hypothek*-ownership of the pledge until the debt is paid[10]. Menes worked from this insight to take the shemittah as a release in which the creditor lost nothing, because he had already gained more than his original loan by use of the pledge (whether farmland or slave); and Koschaker supported him by taking Akkadian *manzazânu* as *antichresis*-pledge[11].

Weil thereupon argued chiefly from use in Deut 15,2 of the term *nāgaš*, "force to labor, impose *corvée*", as Pharaoh in Ex 3,7, seeing in *šāmat massâ* release of the (slave-) gage "as a concrete object [not excluding a living person], not an abstract debt". Our view was not exactly supported by Weil's two claims that the "pledge" was not the debtor himself but a member of his family (though both equally relate to the preservation of family-property), and that the pledge is delivered only when the debt falls due, not at the time of making the contract.

Chirichigno notes these differences, and also the substantial similarity of Weil's view to that of Horst. For both, he observes, the release of the pledge was identical to the total remission of the debt. He names six more recent experts who share this view. But he then details his reasons for not being able to admit that Deut 15,2 can refer to a human pledge. At the end he stresses that unlike us he maintains that Deut 15,2 proposes a kind of release which is different from that of Lev 25,4.

Pfandrecht", *Welt des Orients* 8 (1975; 218-227) p. 227 admits only *Ersatzpfand*: not *Eigentumspfand*; see also his "Zum altbabylonischen Pfandrecht", *Zeitschrift der Savigny-Stiftung für Rechtsgeschichte* 83 (1966) 334-8.

[9] Gregory C. CHIRICHIGNO, *Debt-Slavery in Israel and the Ancient Near East* (1989 diss.: JSOT supp. 141 (Sheffield 1993) 267-273 on pledge not envisioned in Deut 15,1-3; and his p. 73-85.97 on pledge in Mesopotamia. His p.266 equates Weil's "pledge" with that of F. HORST in *Gottes Recht* (1949 = 1961) p. 192-4. E.NEUFELD, "Inalienability .. of Pledges", *RIDA* 3/9 (1962) p. 33-44, holds the pledge was only a means of putting pressure on debtor.

[10] Max WEBER, "Agrarverhältnisse im Altertum", *Gesammelte Aufsätze zur Sozial- und Wirtschaftsgeschichte* (Tübingen 1924) 87. Hence my formulation "every debt is a form of *antichrēsis*" in "Jubileo", *Enciclopedía Bíblica* (Barcelona 1963, Garriga) p. 710.

[11] Abram MENES, *Die vorexilischen Gesetze Israels*: BZAW 50 (1928), p.81; Paul KOSCHAKER, "Über ... Eigentums- und Pfandbegriff", *Annalen der sächsischen Akademie ph/h* 42/1 (1931) p. 17.

Suitable note of Weil is taken also by Cholewiński (p. 95 below), who not only shares my favor but attributes it also to Cazelles and others. Merendino in fact notes that *šāmaṭ* nowhere else is used with persons as object [though the point at issue above was rather whether the object is the debt itself or the concrete reality of the pledge][12]. Cholewiński's p. 222 further tries to conciliate the seventh year ("after the sixth") of Ex 21,2 (and 23,12) and even of Deut 15,12, with Deut 15,1 "at the *end* of every *seventh* year" via Jer 34,14, debt-slave release "in seventh year, after six" decreed by King Zedekiah, but reneged[13].

According to Finet, the Mari *kiššatum* means both gage and subjection; but if the gage was in silver or money, it was called *nipûtum*[14].

The curious notion that a wager or bet was sometimes taken to be determinative for the fate of a pledge (or even debt) has been found to be hinted in 2 Kgs 18,23 (= Isa 36,8)[15].

4. The Jubilee compilation of earlier debt-treatments

Chaney endeavors to link discordant elements in traditional Israel debt-laws with the phases of its history. "Leviticus 25,8-55 is a literarily composite complex of debt-easement law. Whether or not the factional conflict occasioning its promulgation involved a royal figure, as did the related texts in Exodus [Jeroboam/Hezekiah] and Deuteronomy [Josiah], its concerns probably witness a priestly elite disputing jurisdiction over land, peasant production, and cult [clue: 49 years is about how long after Cyrus's 538 decree it would have taken Sheshbazzar to organize an arrival in Judah]. The espousal of traditions of debt easement by the returnees would have

---

[12] Alfred CHOLEWIŃSKI, *Heiligkeitsgesetz und Deuteronomium. Eine vergleichende Studie*: Analecta Biblica 66 (Rome 1976) 219n18; p.223 cites Rosario P. MERENDINO, *Das deuteronomische Gesetz*: BonnerBB 31 (1969) p.108: Ex 23,11 & Jer 17,4 have land-heritage as object; Deut 15,4-6 (if the law is observed, there will be no needy in Israel) held post-deuteronomic. Note that he is speaking of the shemitta *šmṭ* (with dot under *ṭ*); the *šᵉmitut* (with dot under *s* but not under *t*, as in LORETZ p.44n3) is used only (Lev 25,23.30) for things.

[13] Nahum SARNA, "Zedekiah's Emancipation of Slaves and the Sabbatical Year (Jer 34,12-16)" in C. GORDON Fest. *Orient and Occident*.ed. H. HOFFNER: AOAT 22 (Kevelaer/Neukirchen 1973) 143-9.

[14] André FINET, "Le 'gage' et la 'sujétion' (*nipûtum* et *kiššatum*) dans les textes de Mari et le Code de Hammurabi", *Akkadica* 8 (1978) 12-18.

[15] Ze'ev FALK, *Hebrew Law in Biblical Times: an Introduction* (Jerusalem 1964, Wahrmann), p. 102.

struck deep resonance in the peasants"[16].

McConville finds in the Deut 15,13 insistence that the owner provide liberally for the released "slave" a proof that this formulation was later and more "liberal" than that of Ex 21[17]. Japhet goes further aiming to show that its "liberality" is even later than the Holiness-Law version in Leviticus[18]. So also Wright in *God's People*); Lasserre adds that Deut refers to the Ex parallel but does not cite it as a law; what is required is an owners' change in perspective[19].

Further insistence of this pericope that "the service which the debt-slave has given for six years was the *mišneh* of a hired man's salary" (Deut 15,18) has given rise to considerable perplexity and controversy. The Hebrew term usually means "double", and some exegetes have tried to show how the services of a debt-tenant have at least surpassed, if not actually doubled, those of a free employee[20]. But against this view Tsevat has defended his previous and more appropriate claim that as in Akkadian *mišneh* can mean also "equivalent"[21].

---

[16] Marvin L. CHANEY, "Debt Easement in Israelite History and Tradition", in Festschrift N. GOTTWALD, *The Bible and the Politics of Exegesis,* ed. D, JOBLING, *al.* (Cleveland 1991, Pilgrim; 127-139), p. 137-8; citing in n.4.5.30 also his "Systemic Study of the Israelite Monarchy", *Semeia* 37 (1986) 60-74 & "Ancient Palestine Peasant Movements and the Formation of Premonarchic Israel", in D.N. FREEDMAN, D.F. GRAF, ed., *Palestine in Transition: the Emergence of Ancient Israel*: Social World of Biblical Antiquity 2 (Sheffield 1983) 52-57.72-83.

[17] J.G. MCCONVILLE, *Law and Theology in Deuteronomy* (diss. Belfast 1980: JSOT.S 33, Sheffield 1984) p. 97. CHIRICHIGNO (ftn. 9 above) p.184 reference to female "captive" is doubtless in a wide sense: see p. 60 above.

[18] Sara JAPHET, "The Laws of Manumission of Slaves and the Question of Relationship between the Collections of Laws in the Pentateuch", in Fest. S.E. LOEWENSTAMM, *Studies in the Bible and Ancient Near East,* ed. Yitschak AVISHUR & Joshua BLAU (Jerusalem 1978, Rubinstein), Eng. vol. p. 199-200 (Heb. vol. 231-250); further "The Relation between the Legal Corpora of the Pentateuch in the Light of the Manumission Laws", *Scripta Hierosolymitana* 31 (1986) 63-89.

[19] Christopher J.H. WRIGHT, *God's People in God's Land: Family, Land. and Property in the Old Testament* (Grand Rapids/Exeter 1990, Eerdmans/Paternoster) p. 142; Guy LASSERRE, "LUTHER contre la paupérisation et ses conséquences; lecture rhétorique de Dt 15/12-28", *Études Théologiques et Religieuses* 70 (1993) 481-492.

[20] James M. LINDENBERGER, "How Much for a Hebrew Slave ? The meaning of *mišneh* in Deut 15:18", *JBL* 110 (1991) 479-482: "double" but just an exaggeration.

[21] Mattatiahu TSEVAT, "The Hebrew Slave according to Deuteronomy 15:12-18: his Lot and the Value of his Work, with Special Attention to the Meaning of *mišneh*", *JBL* 113 (1994) 587-595, as already in *HUCA* 29 (1955) 125.

5. *Mešarum and current status of Mesopotamian parallels*

The biblical outlook on slavery, even if debt-"slavery", doubtless owes much to Mesopotamian uses. Cardellini devotes more than half his book to these, in chronological order and under the name of the ruler, not the subject decreed. His biblical research is chiefly on ("H") Lev 25,39-55 with briefer advertence to Jer 34,8-22 and Neh 5,1-13; all preceded and followed by comparison with Ex 21 and Deut 15[22].

The proportion of space allotted to Mesopotamia in Chirichigno 1993 is almost equally long. The relevant chapter 2 in my 1954 dissertation pays due attention to *andurarum;* also *muškenum* and *biltum*, which now form the object of one of Kraus's collected essays[23].

But we had no access to *mešarum*, which was catapulted to prominence by the seven examples in one edict published by Kraus. Though it literally means "(maintain) the existing good order" it actually promulgates a release of debts[24]. A further sample of *mešarum* (which is often spelled *mišarum*)

---

[22] Innocenzo CARDELLINI, *Die biblischen "Sklaven"-Gesetze im Lichte des keilschriftlichen Sklavenrechts*: BonnBB 55, 1981: p. 1-229, Mesopotamia (excursus on *muškēnum* p.91; no *andurarum*, but see *dᵉrôr* p.282, n.221); -- p. 286-311, Lev 25,39-55; 312-322, Jer 34,8-22; 323-335, Neh 5,1-13. See now his 1999 article (p.21, ftn.1).

[23] F.R. KRAUS, *Vom mesoptamischen Menschen der altbabylonischen Zeit und seiner Welt. Eine Reihe Vorlesungen*: Mededelingen Ned. Akad.; Lett. NR 36,6 (Amsterdam 1973, North-Holland), p. 95-117 (= p. 291-313). Further Edward LIPIŃSKI, "Sale, Transfer, and Delivery in Ancient Semitic Terminology", in H. KLENGEL, *Gesellschaft und Kultur im Vorderasien* (Berlin 1982, Akademie; 173-185), p. 198 on *muškenu*: "palace-man (royal functionary" in I. KLÍMA, "Im ewigen Banne der *muškēnum*-Problematik", in J. HARMATTA & G. KOMORÓCZY, ed., *Wirtschaft* (1976) 267-274. In LEMCHE *VTS* 37 (1985; p.77n9) p. 167 *muškenu* seems to be equated with *ḫupšu*, "client". -- More widely, Johannes RENGER, "On Economic Structures in Ancient Mesopotamia", *Orientalia* 63 (1994) 157-208, critique of Morris SILVER, partially on DOUGLASS NORTH.

[24] F.R. KRAUS, *Ein Edikt des Königs Ammi-Ṣaduqa von Babylon*: SDOAP 5 (Leiden 1958) Brill) p. 242; on p. 229 N° 44 is his dating of *this* edict, referred to p. 106, the Ammi-Saduqa datings with sigla "17+c". -- N.P. LEMCHE, "*Andurarum* and *mišarum*: comments on the problem of social edicts and their application in the ancient Near East", *JNES* 38 (1979) 11-22; H. OLIVIER, "The Effectiveness of the Old Babylonian *Mēšarum* Decree", *Journal of North-West Semitic Languages* 12 (1984) 107-113: inscription AB 5 273 shows it was hard on business and on the lender; so J. BOTTÉRO, "Désordre économique et annulation des dettes en Mésopotamie à l'époque paléo-babylonienne", *JESHO* 4 (1961) 113-164.

was later published by Kraus and both were commented by Finkelstein[25], in the second of which he discussed the important issue of possible periodicity of the edict[26]. Kraus took up further elswhere the *simdat šarrim*, "(royal) sending"[27].

The experts are generally careful to acknowledge the extent to which Mesopotamian (and Egyptian) similarities are not provably more than verbal, rather than real parallels or especially origins of the biblical expressions. But Phillips finds it necessary to call attention to Talmon's warning that the comparative method is useful only after the meaning has been established from within the biblical text[28]. Phillips also revises in accord with Lemche his previous view relating Deut 15,12-18 to Deut 15,1-11

6. Relationship of girl-"slaves" to debt

It has aroused exegetes' concern that some of the laws with which we have been dealing treat as a special problem the fate to be accorded to the wives or daughters of debtors, while others make no distinction. In principle of course the working out of debt did not concern the women-folk, since (with due attention to the prominent case of Zelophehad in Num 36), they were normally not property-owners, and matters of debt would concern rather their husbands or fathers. But there remains the intriguing question of whether Israelite girls who had been sold into some kind of "slavery"-arrangement were to regain their freedom through a *gô'ēl* or the occurrence of a Jubilee.

The principal and rather complex relevant passage is Ex 21, 3-4 & 7-11. We will begin with Ex 21,7, whose formulation is sure to give offense nowadays: "When a man sells his daughter as a slave ... " -- which it is

---

[25] F.R. KRAUS, "Ein Edikt des Königs Samsu-ilumas von Babylon", *Assyriologische Studien* 16 (1965) 225-231; J.J. FINKELSTEIN, (Duplikat in) *RAss* 63 (1969) 45-64.189; & "Some new *misharum* Material and its Implications", *Assyriologische Studien* 16 (1965) 233-246.

[26] G. KOMORÓCZY, "Zur Frage der Periodicität des altbabylonischen *mišarum*", in Fest. I. DIAKONOFF, *Societies and Languages of the Ancient Near East*, ed. M.A. DANDAMAYEV, (Warminster 1982, Aris & Phillips), p. 196-205.

[27] F. R. KRAUS, *Königliche Verfügungen in altbabylonischer Zeit*: Studia et Documenta ad Iura Orientis Antiqui Pertinentia 11 (Leiden 1984, Brill) p.8.

[28] Anthony PHILLIPS, "The Law of Slavery: Exodus 21.2-11", *JSOT* 30 (1984; 51-66) 54; Shemaryahu TALMON, "The 'Comparative Method' in Biblical Interpretation -- Principles and Problems". *Congress Volume, Göttingen 1977*: VTS 29 (1978) 320-356.

made clear he has a perfect right to do; perhaps but not clearly implied even to a non-Israelite, though she and her father are both evidently Israelites.

The passage continues, equally or even more offensively, "she shall not go free as male slaves do": unlike Deut 15,17 "Your female slave also you shall treat in the same way" -- though only for her renouncement of liberation, as noted below.

But there is food for reflection in the beginning of Ex 21,8, "But if her master, who had destined her for himself" ("as a wife of second rank", the New American Bible inserts; and that is of course one of the possibilities; in the light of recorded biblical facts one might even use the still more repugnant expression "concubine").

But I see nothing in the wording or in any parallels to exclude that she is intended to be the first or only wife of the buyer. The word "sale" though not repeated here, is of course out of place by today's standards. But we are all aware that through history marriage was frequently accompanied by a money exchange, often legally documented, just as the "dowry" in the opposite direction[29]. Re-reading in this light all the biblical passages mentioning the sale of daughters, one is tempted to conclude that this is sometimes or normally the means of acquiring a wife -- honorably, indeed more so than by some other devices.

And obviously in such a case, "she shall not go free, as male slaves do", Ex 21,7. However, that same verse 8 which had opened out the possibility of her financially-accompanied choice as marriage-partner, adds several complex clauses protecting her in case of what we today call "divorce for incompatibility". First, her buyer "shall let her be redeemed" by a *gô'ēl* relative if she is so fortunate as to have one (and we elsewhere cited the observation that strangely the father himself is nowhere indicated as *gô'ēl*) or by the resources eventually to be revised and harmonized in Lev 25.

"He cannot sell her to a foreigner" hints that perhaps this had not been excluded in her pre-marital sale as noticed above. And the specially significant reason is added, "because this would be a breach-of-promise" [Jerusalem Bible; or even better NAB "he has broken faith with her"]. This

---

[29] Grace I. EMMERSON, "Women in Ancient Israel", in *The World of Ancient Israel*, ed. R.E. CLEMENTS (Cambridge 1989, Univ.; 371-394; 388s, "Women and slavery"), p. 380 on Ex 22,15 (seducer bound to marry with customary payment) prefers "marriage-present" for *môhār* (elsewhere only Gen 34,12; 1 Sam 18,25) to "brideprice" of DE VAUX and NEUFELD; her p. 393 cites A. BRENNER, *The Israelite Woman; Social Role and Literary Type in Biblical Narrative*: Biblical Seminar 2 (Sheffield 1985, JSOT) and M. EVANS, *Woman in the Bible* (Exeter 1983, Paternoser).

comment, though a little late in arriving, sheds a strong backward light supportive of our view that in many other cases beside this one where divorce ensued, the daughter was really "given as a bride" -- though along with financial considerations not unlike those that have been customary through the ages.

Ex 21,9, hopefully fitting retroactively between "destined her ... for himself; dislikes her", opens out even from the beginning the more acceptable option that the bride was acquired not for the "buyer" himself but for his son, equivalently a new daughter for himself, to be honored as such.

If, as was common in that polygamous background, he took another wife, then there was hope that the prior one would retrieve her freedom without cost (other than that of being no longer so nubile), unless the husband continued to provide the three essentials of the marriage-bond on which we found some obscurity in Ex 21,10-11[30].

A different type of feminine relevance is prominent in Ex 21,3-6. "If (the 'purchased slave') comes into service alone, he shall leave alone; if he comes with a wife, his wife shall leave with him. But if his 'buyer' gives him a wife and she bears him sons or daughters, the woman and the children shall remain the buyer's property and the man shall leave alone". This is a hard saying, and (unless this be regarded as an other wife) ill-compatible with Gen 2,24.

On the other hand, an almost romantic loverliness shines through the assumption of Ex 21,5 that (in part at least) out of attachment to his wife and children the man will choose to remain in slavery forever, by the peculiar ear-piercing ritual of Ex 21,6. With no real support from the biblical text, it has been claimed that even this "forever" is ended by the Jubilee[31].

There is a briefer reference to this ritual in Deut 15,17, with no implication that his motivation is love of the wife of his enslavement. On the contrary, the female slave (not indicated whether already married or still

---

[30] R. NORTH, "Flesh, Covering, and Response, Ex. xi 10", *VT* 5 (1955) 204-6.

[31] Robert GNUSE, *You shall not Steal: Community and Property in the Biblical Tradition.* Maryknoll 1985, Orbis), p. 25 (under Jubilee, "fifty rather than six" though mentioning "after six years)", citing Isaac MENDELSOHN, *Slavery in the Ancient Near East* (NY 1949, Oxford and/or same title "BAR 3" p. 145), p. 143.

single or either) is in this passage subject to the same arrangement as the male -- thus supplying a deficit of Ex 21,7, but only for the free renunciation of her freedom.

7. Conclusions

"Debt, unpayable debt" is really the subject of this chapter, though it is often described by terms which in the Bible sometimes mean slavery, but can mean things quite different, and never as in Roman or American practice. The Bible shows intense concern to preserve the small farmer's independence in face of mounting debts. But it may be suspected that as today the bulk of the population preferred to be job-holder or tenant-farmer and thus spared many of the insecurities and discomforts of ownership.

The biblical expression "Hebrew slave" has been widely claimed to reflect a cognate cuneiform *ḥapiru*, meaning really belonging neither to a specific race nor to a way of earning one's living, but to a group living precariously on the fringes of society and thus seen as a kind of threat to an established order. But insofar as this term is really reflected in "Hebrew", it may refer not to any kind of slavery at all but to their gradual or violent takeover of the land of the Canaanites.

In many cases of unpayable debt, "slave" seems to have somewhat the force of "pledge" ("live-gage" instead of mort-gage) by which the creditor could gradually or somehow be reimbursed ("antichresis").

Perhaps the commonest view among exegetes is that Ex 21, related to the Covenant-Code, gives us the earliest tradition about mercy to debt-victims; and that during the Kings era such provisions in Deut 15 were revised to be made more practicable. Later *all* the preceding traditions were unified by Lev 25 into a kind of simultaneity and organized structurally into some stage of the Holiness Code (before or after the rest of "P"). But there is a recent trend to find in Deut 15 a more liberal and therefore later formulation than those of Lev 25.

Though we are warned against too hastily assuming that the biblical demands of mercy to debt-victims are borrowed from various Mesopotamian prototypes, it is generally admitted that these "parallels" have some relevance, especially the recently-researched *mešarum*. But it is usually stressed that debt-release in Mesopotamia is once-for-all and linked to a new reign, rather than recurrent as in the Bible.

Explicit provision for women is rare in laws made for relief of debtors. But there is occasional approval of the "sale of daughters into slavery", which (taking into account the financial accompaniment of marriage through the centuries) may perhaps imply merely "given as a bride". Special concern is shown for decent treatment of such a bride if she is later rejected. Freedom granted or purchased for a debtor includes a wife whom he already had, and her children; but not a family acquired during his disfranchisement. In this case, he can keep her only if he chooses to continue his subjection forever by recourse to an antique ear-piercing rite -- "because he loves his wife" as is sometimes added.

vii

Cities

We now have two books of identical titles and almost identical author surnames, but of strikingly different approach, to give us the needed background for an exposition of the sections on cities in Leviticus 25,29-34.

1. The City in Ancient Israel

The spankingly modern and well-presented volume by Fritz gives valuable and virtually exhaustive data on all the Canaan-area cities known by excavation, backed by his own experience at Kinneret[1]. Pre-Israel cities flourished from 3000 to 2350; and, after a lapse, then from 2000 to 1150; "the visible break is consistent with an upheaval in political circumstances" (p.44); there is no mention of Joshua-era Israel in this connection (but see his p.12; and in general the Bible is cited often enough to warrant an Index). Four types of available extrabiblical written records are indispensable but not enough for a real history of the cities (p.40).

It is rather casually mentioned on p. 76 that [from 1150] until 1000 there were many villages rather than cities, and on p.173 and 189 that in the Kings era (especially since no craftsmen's workshops have been discovered in the cities, p. 183), it was rather from within cities that most of the dwellers went out to work their farms during the day.

This presumption seems rather at variance with recent excavators'-surveys showing many Iron Age villages[2]. In any case, it is not denied that

---

[1]   Volkmar FRITZ, *The City in Ancient Israel*: Biblical Seminar 29   (Sheffield 1995, Academic; 197 p.; 60 plans). Kinneret ('Oreime) p. 83-87.

[2]   Moshe KOCHAVI, "The Israelite Settlement in Canaan in the Light of Archaeological Surveys", *Biblical Archaeology Today*, Jerusalem Congress 1984 (Jerusalem 1985, Israel Exploration Society; 54-60): p.55, in LB there were no small surface villages, but with the Iron Age they appear by the hundreds.

these city-dwellers were such "independent small landowning farmers" as my present volume claims to be the sole focus of concern in Lev 25, or that the taxes (not a concern of Lev 25) increasing during the monarchy would have afflicted them too. Nevertheless it may be noted that the biblical text and most exegetes seem vaguely to presume that the farmers are actually living on the piece of land they are tilling.

Fritz's excavated data on cities are abundant and presented in many elegant plans, though these often contain dense sections in only small parts of the given area, and no inserts to help pick out and appraise the items focused in the text. All in all it may be said that Fritz gives us rather a history of excavations than a history of cities or analysis of their origin and nature; especially since his occasional brief history-summaries admit that there *must* have been, as in Mesopotamia from much earlier, some kind of written receipts or account books which if found would be of great help.

Altogether different and more akin to our own present interests is the approach in Frick's modestly presented 1977 dissertation[3]. He does not ignore excavation (devoting a special bibliography to it and making a big new point on p. 175 of the urbanization of neolithic Jericho several millennia ahead of its time), but neither does he make archeology specially noticeable. His p.85 claim that the cities had no streets but only unplanned spaces used rather for refuse dumps than for transit, would be his main (tacit) head-on confrontation with Fritz's description of orderly streets heading downward toward the city gate and thus providing an excellent drainage-system: Frick perhaps overlooked his own p. 179 on the street-planned drainage of Tirzah.

Frick begins with a meaty survey of the history of city-research, frankly acccpting religion as the outset-point of pioneer Fustel recognized also by Sjoberg[4]. But his definition of the city is taken rather from the ten points of Childe, which he sets forth partly in the terms of Lampard and corrects

---

[3]   Frank S. FRICK, *The City in Ancient Israel* (Princeton diss. 1970; SBL diss. 36. Missoula 1977, Scholars): I. Urban Studies; II. Etymology; III. The OT City (including Rural-Urban typology); IV. Its Valuation.

[4]   Numa D. FUSTEL DE COULANGES, *The Ancient City, a Study on the Religions, Laws and Institutions of Greece and Rome* [< *La Cité antique* (1864)], tr. Willard SMALL (1875; NY 1982, Dillingham) p.126. -- Gideon SJOBERG, *The Preindustrial City, Past and Present* (Glencoe IL 1960, Free Press) 327; 256-284. -- See further C.R. KRAELING & R. M. ADAMS, ed., *The City Invincible: a Symposium on Urbanization and Cultural Development in the Ancient Near East.* Chicago 1960, Univ.;   A. VAN SELMS, "Die Stad in die Israelitiese voorstellingslewe", *Hervormeerde Teologiese Studies* 8 (Pretoria 1952) 79.

chiefly by requiring defense-walls[5]. To exegetes Childe's most surprising requirements may be "full-time specialists (also in art!)"; "the presence of writing and numerical notation (arithmetic, astronomy)" almost unknown in Canaan before 800, though common in Mesopotamia two millennia earlier!; and "taxes", fairly obvious though unmentioned in Lev 25.

Not only taxes, but all city-dwellers' daily food constitute what Frick p.14 calls "the problem of motivating farmers to (produce a surplus and) surrender food to urbanites". But a more immediate problem is whether the farmers actually lived outside the cities (but belonged to them as a place of *refuge* in case of attack) or rather as Frick more frequently seems to presume, mostly lived *within* the cities and thus had a tedious slow work-animal drive to their place of toil for some tiring wasted hours of each day.

This problem is remotely faced by Frick on p.92 pointing out that the villages really *belonged* to the cities (as "daughters") in a way clarified chiefly by Lev 25,29-34; though in Josh 21,11 they are separated from the cities by the quite-different *pasture* lands. A cognate problem that seems nowhere mentioned by exegetes or city-analysts is whether or what proportion of the city-dwelling farmers were in fact tenants rather than farm-owners.

Frick's final chapter on OT valuation of the city turns out to be largely on prophets' denunciations; thus of less usefulness to us than his detailed comparison of the biblical city's structure and function with the data of more general studies of urbanization, usually rather overlooked by exegetes.

Frick has also a later much more sophisticated and technical essay on agricultural villages around 1200 B.C. with a map, which will be of help to us in struggling to determine the proportion of farmers (owner or tenant) who lived in unwalled villages and not in cities during the pre-Kings era[6]. He relies largely on meteorological and especially anthropological data

---

[5] V. Gordon CHILDE, "The Urban Revolution", *Town Planning Review* 21 (1950) 3-17. - Eric LAMPARD, "Historical Aspects of Urbanization", in P.M. HAUSER & L.F. SCHNORE, ed., *The Study of Urbanization* (NY 1965, Wiley) p. 521; 542. Ten differing points are given by Charles L. REDMAN, *The Rise of Civilization: From Early Farmers to Urban Society in the Ancient Near East* (San Francisco 1978, Freeman) p. 218.

[6] F.S. FRICK, "Ecology, Agriculture and Patterns of Settlement", in *The World of Ancient Israel: Sociological, Anthropological and Political Perspectives*, ed. R. E. CLEMENTS (Cambridge 1989, Univ.; 67-93), map p. 89 from L.E. STAGER, "The Archaeology of the Family in Ancient Israel", *BASOR* 260 (1985; 1-35), p. 2. -- See also C.H.J. DE GEUS, "The Profile of an Ancient City", *Biblical Archaeologist* 49 (1986) 224-227.

"neglected by exegetes"[7]. But regrettably the exegete will not find here the concrete statements he is seeking relative to the proportion of latifundists, small-farm owners, their buyers-out by temporary owners, and tenants (by debt or choice) -- as against artisans and administrative personnel -- dwelling in the cities rather than in these proliferating villages.

The recent *Oxford History of the Biblical World* claims on its p. x special attention to the "tension bewteen rural and urban settings". In fact in the subject-index there is no entry "rural" and under "urbanization" nothing for the years between 2000 and 900. Stager's ch.3, "Forging an Identity: the Emergence of Ancient Israel" has a subtitle "A Ruralization Hypothesis" to account for the proliferation of agricultural villages in the Canaan area after 1200; but his corresponding "Urban Imposition" focuses the Philistines and their economy, rather far southwest of our Canaanite-area center of interest[8].

2. Substantial contribution of Lemche's "Ancient Israel"

Our concern with the coexistence of farm-villages alongside cities forms really a major portion of Lemche's large book aimed primarily at the refutation of Gottwald's "violent peasant revolution" due ultimately to a theory of village and city as anti-morphemes. Is it really true that there was a natural or existing hostility between farmers and city-dwellers, especially if and after most of the farmers were actually living in cities ?

Lemche's first and intended basic subjection of this theory to concrete cases, hopefully entitled "I. Village and City I. Examples; II. Interaction

---

[7] Barbara J. PRICE, "Secondary State Formation: an Explanatory Model", in *Origins of the State*, ed. R. COHEN & E.R. SERVICE (Philadelphia 1978, Institute for the Study of Human Issues), p. 161-186; W.T. SANDERS & D. WEBSTER, "Unilineality, Multilineality, and the Evolution of Complex Societies", in *Social Archaeology*, ed. C.L. REDMAN *al.* (New York 1978, Academic), p. 249-302.

[8] Lawrence E. STAGER, "Forging an Identity; the Emergence of Ancient Israel" in *The Oxford History of the Biblical World*, Michael D. COOGAN, ed. (13 authors; New York 1998, Oxford Univ. Press; 123-173) p.141; 165; see also Stager's "Israelite Settlement in Canaan", in Jerusalem congress *Biblical Archaeology Today*, ed. Amihai MAZAR (Jerusalem 1985, Israel Exploration Soc,) 83-87; "The Impact of the Sea Peoples (1185-1050 BCE)" in *The Archaeology of Society in the Holy Land*. ed. Thomas E. LEVY. (New York 1995, Facts on File) 332-348. Stager's Forging p. 141 cites also Evsey DOMAR, ed., *Capitalism, Socialism, and Serfdom*. New York 1989, Cambridge Univ. Press.

between City and Country" ends up limited to six modern Arab villages on which material has been published[9].

He is forced to this because "despite the fact that two thirds of the population of the Orient are peasants, they have not caught the imagination of early [i.e. two full millennia later] European travellers in the same fashion as the picturesque nomads and the 'mysterious' Oriental cities have done" (p.165), admitting "it would be unreasonable to maintain that ancient Oriental peasant societies were basically the same as existing [Islamized!] ones". From available contemporary data Lemche can hope at most "to avoid a number of fallacious concepts".

But frankly a careful reading of these pages plunges us fully into the atmosphere of Arabic studies, fascinating no doubt but worlds different from the 1000 B.C. Canaan with which we were concerned. And his main "Conclusion" on p. 185 is "it is risky to apply stereotyped generalization. ... There is no distinct borderline between tribally and non-tribally organized peasant societies ... We must unconditionally demand that scholars investigate a given society on its own terms rather than on the basis of some general conception of the ways societies at a particular cultural level behave. In conjunction with ancient Israel, this means that one must attempt to describe its social structure and its economic and political life on the basis of the sources [written or archeological] we happen to possess".

Though he here adds that the written sources are mainly OT, he next gives several pages on Mesopotamian and Syrian cities. Written materials of Ugarit and Alalaḫ are mostly in the terms of Liverani and Lapidus[10]. None of this adds notably to our awareness of village-city coexistence.

Lemche's most useful contribution is perhaps the two subsections p.392-405 entitled "Settlement Pattern II. The Cities; III. The Villages". He begins by noting that in the Early Iron Age (including presumably Canaan 1200-1000) Samaria area undefended villages increased by 600%, often rather concentrated in bunches. He shows only slight concern for whether this relative diminution of prosperity had anything to do with the entry or

---

[9] Niels Peter LEMCHE, *Early Israel. Anthropological and Historical Studies on the Israelite Society Before the Monarchy*: VTS 37 (Leiden 1985, Brill) p. 164-184.

[10] M. LIVERANI, "Communautés de village et palais royal dans la Syrie du IIème millénaire", *JESHO* 18 (1975) 146-164 (ftn. 16 below) and twenty further articles of his cited on Lemche's p.459. -- I.M. LAPIDUS, ed. *Middle Eastern Cities: a Symposium on Ancient, Islamic and Contemporary Middle Eastern Urbanism,* Berkeley 1969.

emergence of a different population ("Israel" for example)[11]. And he strangely shows no concern at all for what proportion of the occupants of the soon-developing big cities were farmers whether independent or tenant[12].

His next chapter, on "The Villages" has to admit that the materials have been inadequately published except for faraway Negeb Masos[13]. But he gets help from Aharoni's Teleil, Kochavi's Izbet Sarta of Canaanite alphabet fame, and Callaway's 'Ai. In the interpretation of most of these sites he regrets "preconceived" Israel occupation, especially in Fritz who must make it *prior* to the results at Masos. Actually whether Canaanite or Israelite is irrelevant to what archeology has to tell us about the *number* of villages in relation to cities, and thus eventually to where the farmers lived: which is important for Lev 25,29-34 even though we cannot with confidence assign to this material a date nearer to 1200 than to 600.

Further researches into the frequency of unwalled village settlements between 1200 and 1000 have been published with a view to determining whether Gottwald's violent or Mendenhall's non-violent peasant uprising marks the outset of "Israel". In some of these both the protagonists take part[14]. They leave largely untouched the problem of what proportion of the (owner or tenant) farmers lived in cities.

3. Where did all the farmers live ?

"*Walled* towns, typical of Canaanite city culture, were a novelty to the

---

[11]   John E. STAMBAUGH, "Cities", *AnchorBD* 1 (1992; 1031-1048) on p. 1036 has a subsection entitled "The Decline of the Canaanite City" followed by "Emergence of the Israelite City", doubtless reflecting a presumption fairly common until recently.

[12]   Bernhard LANG, "The Social Organization of Peasant Poverty in Biblical Israel", *JSOT* 24 (1982; 47-63) p. 50: often and typically "the landowner is a townsman so that the dualism of rich and poor corresponds to the country's dependence on the city" is contrary not only to Lemche's view but also to the likelihood discussed below, that many or most of the farm-workers lived in the cities. His bibliography cites Oswald LORETZ, "Die prophetische Kritik des Rentenkapitalismus", *Ugarit-Forschungen* 7 (1975) 271-8.

[13]   But Kochavi (ftn. 2 above) above and Amihai Mazar there p. 62 hesitantly doubt that Masos was an Israelite site.

[14]   Notably Mendenhall more fiercely and Gottwald rather serenely in David N. FREEDMAN & David F. GRAF ed., *Palestine in Transition; the Emergence of Ancient Israel*: Social World of Biblical Antiquity 2 (Sheffield 1983, Almond/ASOR) p. 91-103 & 25-37; but the main presentation is by M. CHANEY p. 39-90. -- Also Alan J. HAUSER, "Israel's Conquest of Palestine: a Peasants' Rebellion" (p.2-19), with Mendenhall (28-34), Gottwald (37-52), and T. THOMPSON (20-27) in *JSOT* 7 (1978).

Israelite farming population and their customary family law did not provide for them. So a house in such a town was considered more an individual than a family possession. ... But the agricultural Israelites were used to living in *unwalled hamlets*, so houses there were treated as landed property, and the old rules applied. The Levites, however, formed a special case. Whatever their past history may have been, by the time of the exile, which is the situation here, the Levites had become a group of ministers performing certain duties in connection with the sanctuary, but distinct from, and subordinate to, the priesthood proper ... At some period, probably toward the end of the monarchy, they had acquired a number of towns in which to reside (Josh 21) ... towns regarded as a gift from the Israelites to the whole Levitical group"[15].

This comment on Lev 25,29 may well serve as a summary of the problems to be treated in this chapter; though without claiming we know more than we do about the exact dating of the various sections, whether exilic or postexilic or ancient preserved fragments, as has been variously debated.

It would seem highly probable that to the compiler of Lev 25 the small independent farmer actually lived upon the same plot of land which he tilled. And as far as I can recall, virtually 100% of exegetical treatments of these passages make the same presumption: without drawing from it any conclusions regarding the possibility that some farmers may have lived in cities. Thus Hartley's recent commentary speaks of "the nature of life in a walled city. In these larger cities the population was racially mixed, and the populace did not live off the land" (p.430).

Hartley there states that the racial mix, Canaanites and other resident aliens who lived in the walled cities "were not covered by land inheritance laws of Israel; this exception gave them the right to buy and sell houses within Israelite walled cities", which could be repurchased only within a year and would not be affected by the Jubilee. The restriction of this repurchase right to a single year and without benefit of Jubilee is perhaps an obscure reference to the "racial mix" within the walled cities and to the likelihood that only non-Israelites would have bought such houses.

Elliger's commentary (p.356), unlike Hartley reflecting the urbanization data above, says that already before the Kings era but especially then the

---

[15] J. R. PORTER, *Leviticus*: Cambridge Commentary, 1976, p.202. His p. 197 holds that both the sabbath year [*sic*, not as most "sabbatical"] and the jubilee "certainly" rest on practices attested before the exile.

Israelite populace was largely dwelling within walled cities "and usually mostly as farmers". Among other possibilities, he suggests that the exceptional treatment of walled-city house sale may have been in conformity with "Old-Canaanite city law".

Reflection on the observations mentioned above leads me to reckon with six different possibilities:

(1) The independent small farmer alone lived on his plot and with his family did all the work on it: as seems to be the impression conveyed by all the various parts of Lev 25 except verse 13.

(2) The farmer as long as he was debt-free had one or more tenants who had previously been like himself; or possibly (also) hired employees or workers whom he had acquired among Israelites ('slaves' Lev 25,39) or aliens (Lev 25,45).

(3) The farmer who "temporarily sold" his land (Lev 25,14) because of debt (Lev 25,10) continued to live on it as before, and to till it with his family for an "absentee landlord" presumably living in a city.

(4) The new *pro tem* owner himself lives on the farm and has his own hired staff to till it, so that the former owner must find a place to live and work elsewhere as seems to be the situation implied by Lev 25,13.

(5) The former owner continues to work the property as tenant, but the new owner moves in to live there and supervise the work of his tenant.

(6) Whether the new owner lives there or in a city, the expropriated owner lives in a city but comes out daily to till his former holding as tenant (perhaps accompanied by some of his children or even by his wife; but some of the researches on cities state that inside them there was enough "women's work" like weaving and food-preserving).

We must admit that none of these possibilities seems to be even considered in the text itself or in the hundreds of exegetical researches on it. Why then should we consider important or even worthy of attention details which are not so considered by the text ? Our answer must be that in long reflection on the text and on answers which have been given to the problems it raises, these six possibilities would be of genuine relevance in determining the really envisioned situation which the biblical text aims to relieve.

4. Observations relevant to Leviticus 25 dating

One might be tempted to say that in Lev 25,29 "walled cities" are brought in abruptly out of nowhere, and in relation only to architecture rather than to tilling the soil. But when, as in some of the statements cited above, the exegete is confronted with the claim that *most* farmers lived within the walled cities, and had to waste some hours of every work-day driving their service-animals (past the pasture-lands!) to the site of operations, then one is forced to gave some really serious thought to what view of the matter underlay the formulations chosen by the compiler of Lev 25. Certainly neither he nor any other biblical author ever mentions this as a problem.

One obvious answer which should be considered is that the compiler of Lev 25 was active at the end of the exilic period, and he was not writing about any really existing farm-conditions at all, but only about how the farmlands of Judah would have to be restored to "the block of their former ownership" upon its return from Babylon.

No hint is ever given, either in the biblical texts and exegetes, or in the works of Fritz and Frick and Lemche cited above, as to whether the farmers living within the walled cities were owners of their plots or tenant-farmers. It seems quite likely indeed that Lev 25 supposes that the farmer who has lost his ownership by debt(-"slavery") continued to work the same plot as a tenant and hoped to regain it by the Jubilee. We noticed, indeed, some contrary views such as that the land was henceforth worked not by the expropriated former owner but by the (?go'el-) buyer or by the creditor.

In any case, the proportion of farmers who are declared to dwell within walled cities must have been very largely tenants. This likelihood must make quite a difference in our reading and understanding of the biblical data not only on walled cities but on references to the expropriated farmer in general.

Also, as we noticed above, there is never any reference to the burden of tax, nor to the need and means of producing a surplus of food. The tax would not have been an issue for either of the two periods commonly mentioned as *Sitz im Leben* for the jubilee: the Joshua-era and the portion of the Ezra-era in which the Persian administration and heavy taxing had already begun to function. (The Kings era is taken into account mainly for Deut 15 as a midway stage, or less often for Ex 21 & 23 as a parallel to Mesopotamian kings' usages.)

In either of these periods it might well be assumed that the compiler knew very little of the actual circumstances of what he was writing about. In the Joshua era this could have been due not to any ideology or theorizing; but because, even if he was formulating a genuine law which he seriously intended to be put into practice, still at the moment of settlement it could hardly be foreseen what the circumstances would be like up to 50 years later.

In the Ezra-era, on the other hand, it seems likeliest that the "law" of the whole chapter would have been aimed rather at forcing the actual occupants of Judah to restore the farmland to their former owners, and scraps of traditional practice would have been thrown in with very little concern as to whether actual tillers of the soil were living or were to live in cities, taxed, or as tenants.

In dealing with the alleged "anti-morpheme" between rural and city-dwelling ruling or property-owning classes, we may well note that in Syria the situation was quite different from those discussed above. According to Liverani's research, the villages were inhabited by farmers, whether rich or poor, owner or tenant: these were all called "free citizens". In the cities, on the contrary, dwelt the so-called "King's men", people who did not produce food but performed other services of administration or artisanate[16].

5. What is meant by Levitical Cities ?

The three verses Lev 25,32-34 further extend to cities the Jubilee repurchase rights. Though here there is question of "Levitical" cities rather than walled cities, a glance at a map of the 48 Levitical cities of Josh 21,1-42; 1 Chr 6,54-81 held up beside a city-map of biblical Israel will show that really all the biggest and most important cities are "Levitical". The more recent discussions tend to take this as meaning only that the larger cities required elaborate account-keeping and other administrative chores entrusted to the Levites because of their special fitness. But Faley holds that Levites may have actually been assigned a limited property-ownership in "their" cities[17].

Already to Moses in Moab was given YHWH's command that *walled* cities along with 500 yards of *pasture* land in *each* direction were to be given to the Levites for their dwellings and their flocks, with no mention of farming (Num 35,2-4 cited to Joshua at Shiloh as YHWH's command to Moses, Josh 21,2)[18]. This seems like a fairly idealized advance arrangement whether or not it is inconsistent with the command of Num 18,20 that the sons of Aaron are to have no heritage in the land; the following verses say that the Levites are to have only tithes (no land: Num 36,62; Deut 10.9).

---

[16] Mario LIVERANI, "Communautés de village et palais royal dans la Syrie du IIème millénaire", *JESHO* 18 (1975) 146-164.

[17] Roland J. FALEY, "Leviticus", in *New Jerome Biblical Commentary*, ed. Raymond E. BROWN, *al.* (Englewood Cliffs 1990, Prentice-Hall 61-79) p. 78.

[18] Jacob MILGROM, "The Levitic Town: an Exercise in Realistic Planning", *Journal of Jewish Studies* 33 (1982) 185-8 is mainly concerned with sizing usably the 500-yard (x 4) pasture land.

Albright's study of the Joshua text concludes that (at any rate some 200 years later under David) there really were 48 cities with some Levitical exemptions[19]. It would be interesting to know whether he gave thought to what a hard time the farmers (who as more recent studies claim constituted the walled cities' chief inhabitants) would have had getting their oxen past that pasture-space to their sometimes quite far remote tillable fields.

The Jubilee chapter, in its effort to include and relate (with alterations if necessary) all surviving traditional fragments of social justice legislation, cannot overlook this special situation of the Levites. Chiefly their ample pasture lands are made totally unsalable, without reference to any jubilee or repurchase. Though these pastures were presumably destined for flocks of the Levites, Hartley maintains that because of their religious duties "they are not to be burdened with shepherding; their houses then are their primary possession" on which they have the rights of repurchase (indefinitely, not for just a year) and of Jubilee release.

This immense generosity to the Levites would fit very well the often assumed late/post-exilic situation for a compilation of Leviticus 25 by priestly scribes concerned not about realistic farming problems but with the hope of getting the lands of Judah restored and under priestly leadership.

6. *Conclusions*

The unexpected prominence of cities, both walled and Levitical, in the Jubilee chapter was given slight attention in most commentaries published before 1980. But since then several oustanding researches on the cities and their inhabitants raise questions about the farming population that are very relevant to Leviticus 25.

From excavations focused by these researches it seems quite likely that up to the year 1200 B.C. there were very few rural settlements, but that this number suddenly and enormously increased. One cannot help wondering whether this situation was due to an invasion of "Israel" at this time, or should rather be related to a "peasants' uprising", whether peaceful or violent. But those historical questions are not the issue for our Jubilee research.

---

[19] William F. ALBRIGHT, "The List of Levitic Cities", in *Louis Ginzberg Jubilee Volume*. 1945, p. 49-73; also his *Archaeology and the Religion of Israel* (1942) 121-4; R. BOLING, "Levitical Cities: Archaeology and Texts", in Fest S. IWRY, *Biblical and Related Studies*, ed. A.KORT, S. MIRSCHAUER (Winona Lake IN 1985, Eisenbrauns) 23-32; G. HENTON-DAVIES, "Levitical Cities", *IDB* 3 (1962) 116-7; Zechariah KALLAI, "The System of Levitic Cities: a Historical-Geographical Study in Biblical Historiography", *Zion* 45 (1980) 13-34 in Hebrew.

The surprising question which is raised is whether the farmers really lived on the land which they tilled, or in cities at some distance away. This never before constituted a problem. It seemed fully taken for granted both by the text and by the exegetes that each farmer with his family resided on the little plot of land which he worked.

But some of the recent researches on what the cities were like state quite firmly that they were largely inhabited by farmers, who would thus have to waste some hours each day driving their oxen to their work-place and back. Other city-researches, while leaving out of purview that problem, maintain firmly that the city inhabitants were mostly artisans (of whom excavation has given us very little trace) or administrators.

The farmers' wives, in any case, had within the cities plenty of what used to be called "women's work" like cooking, weaving, food-preserving: though the children from a fairly early age may have had to go along to help with the farm.

Our question turns out to be quite complex when we take into account that the "farmer" may indeed be the one whom Leviticus focuses, the independent small farmer. But the city-dweller may just as well be a farmer reduced by debt to tenant-status; or the alien or other hired men who may have preferred the security of peasant status. Or again it could mean the wealthy "farmer" who bought out the poor man's property and (if he did not opt to till it himself or live on it to supervise his now-tenant) went to live in the city, possibly becoming a "latifundist". All of these are possibilities to take into account in clarifying what the Jubilee "homecoming" would have been (or was intended to be).

The special problem raised by the Levitical cities is not so much the inalienability of the Levites' property which Lev 25,32 regulates, but rather the fact known only from Josh 21: Each of the 48 Levite cities (including virtually all the important cities) was surrounded by 500 yards of pasture-lands (of what good to the Levites?) which could not be used for farming -- but increased somewhat the distance which any city-dwelling farmer would have had to go to get to his farm.

Since many of such problems had never been raised so far, we may hope that future researches on the biblical city will include these in their agenda.

viii

Source-Dissection

The JEPD source-dissection which reigned for a century has recently been challenged in various ways. However, despite or even within these challenges, it has so far continued to maintain a certain usefulness. As is becoming customary, we will refer certain verses to P or others of the sources to which they have been commonly attributed[1], without thereby taking issue on the validity of the hypothesis as a whole.

The entire legal corpus from Ex 21 to Num 10 is in general attributed to P, the Priestly Code. But the chapters 17 to 26 of Leviticus have come to be qualified as H (holiness-code, *Heiligkeitsgesetz*) as a subdivision of P.

1. Elliger's eightfold division based on thou / ye

These prevailing norms have been taken by Elliger as the basis of his source-dissection[2]. It is quite recent and the most complicated, though it seems accepted in its entirety by Meinhold without demur[3]. It recognizes

---

[1] Otto EISSFELDT, *Hexateuch-Synopse* (Darmstadt 1962 = 1922, Wissenschaftliche Buchgesellschaft) is still the quickest way to find these attributions, though account must be taken of divergences which have been proposed or almost universally accepted. Further on JEPD see note 8 below and following.

[2] Karl ELLIGER, *Leviticus*: Handbuch zum Alten Testament (Tübingen 1966, Mohr/Siebeck) 335-337, cited with publishers' kind approval. His eightfold source-dissection is justified in great detail on p.338-347, beginning with the "bridge" and supplementary items Lev 25,23-55, which furnish clues to the ensuing more essential Lev 25,1-22.

[3] Arndt MEINHOLD, "Zur Beziehung Gott, Volk, Land im Jobel-Zusammenhang", *BZ* 29 (1995; 245-261) 251; on p. 258 he says "With the Jubilee-context is developed a theological setting which takes up older views of the land as communal property, linked to the organization of the people in *Sippen* (*mišpaḥôt*, clans. extended families: as H.G.

various Redactors (R) and Glossators, and thus it traces the verses or verse-parts of Leviticus 25 to eight different origins. Among these is assigned also a chronological sequence.

This complexity is not likely to be surpassed, and is even likely to be taken as point of departure for simpler dissections. Hence it can be given detailed notice here without entering into the controversy as to whether it (or the whole JEPD-project) is to be redimensioned or rejected.

We will therefore begin with our own translation of the whole chapter, indicating as Elliger does by different type-fonts his alleged respective "authors". The translation (from the Hebrew) and the subtitles are my own. Instead of "you" are used the archaic "thou" sg., "ye" pl., since his division is largely based on the shift between singular and plural you. Gerstenberger rightly remarks that in a completely unified preaching style it is not unusual to slip from singular to plural (as in Lev 25,17), but he admits that insights can be gained by reading consecutively only the plurals of a passage[4].

Here are Elliger's eight sources, with the type-fonts he uses for each, and our equivalents:

Ordinary (his ordinary antiqua): (P) Heiligkeitsgesetz 1.
Ordinary underlined (his ordinary Gothic): (P) H, second hand.
Double underlined (his Gothic petit): addition by same hand.
Bold-face (his Halbfette Antiqua): Main source of *Vorlage* 1.
Italic double underlined: (Halbfette Bembo v.37)): *Vorlage* 1,older material.
Bold italic (his Bold Gothic): Author of *Vorlage* 1, Jubilee
Bold underlined (his Halbfette Antiqua Petit): *Vorlage* 2, Sabbath Year.
Italic (his ordinary italic): Levite Cities added.

KIPPENBERG, *Religion und Klassenbildung* 1978, p.25; rejected by the compiler of Lev 25 in favor of only YHWH's land-ownership) and strives to use them to normativize future interrelations. There is still nothing (*noch nichts*) to be perceived in Lev 25 of the continuing vagueness of *mišpaḥa* in postexilic times)". Continuing to follow Elliger's commentary, Meinhold's p. 260 holds (against B. UFFENHEIMER's *Shnaton* 1980,15 utopian-eschatological) "Jubilee concepts reach back into the preexilic era and were not an exilic invention -- probably" but "certainly observed in practice" he cites from J.R. PORTER's Cambridge commentary 1976, 197.

    [4] E. GERSTENBERGER, *Leviticus*: ATDeutsch 6 (1993) 340; on p. 344 he notes that the opening passage on the fallow is in several points strangely unreal (*wirklichkeitsfremd*) and considers some suggestions that have been made for getting around this. -- Walter KORNFELD, *Studien zum Heiligkeitsgesetz (Lev 17-26)* (Vienna 1952, Herder) 57 indicates some further discussion of the sg./pl. variation.

I. Seventh-year Fallow

1. And YHWH spoke to Moses on Mount Sinai, saying:

2. "Speak to the children of Israel, and thou shalt say to them, 'When ye shall come into the Land which I am giving to ye, then the Land shall repose a sabbath for YHWH.

3. **Six years thou shalt sow thy field, and six years thou shalt prune thy vineyard and gather its products.**

4. **But in the seventh year, Sabbath of Big Sabbath there shall be for the Land, sabbath for YHWH; thy land thou shalt not sow and thy vineyard thou shalt not prune.**

5. **The extra growth of thy harvest thou shalt not harvest, and the grapes of thy unshorn thou shalt not close off; it shall be a year of Big Sabbath for the Land.**

6. **Then shall the sabbath of the land be for ye for food**, for thee and for thy servant and for thy maid and for thy employee and for thy resident aliens

7. and for thy cattle and for the animals in thy land shall be all the produce for food.

II. The Jubilee Fallow

8. *And thou shalt count for thyself seven sabbaths of years, seven years seven times, and they shall be to thee the days of seven sabbaths of the years, forty-nine years.*

9. *And thou shalt sound the ramshorn of blast in the seventh month on the tenth of the month;* on the Day of the Atonements ye shall sound the ramshorn in all your Land.

10. And ye shall sanctify the year of fifty years, and ye shall proclaim liberation in the land to all its inhabitants; it shall be a jubilee for ye; and ye shall return each man to his property, and each man to his family ye shall return.

11. **Jubilee it is,** the year of the fifty years shall be for ye; ye shall not sow and ye shall not reap its overgrowth and ye shall not close off its unshorn.

12. Because it is Jubilee it shall be holy to ye; from the field ye shall eat its produce.

III. The Jubilee Homecoming

13. In this Jubilee year shall ye **each again come to his property.**

14. **And if** *'thou sellest' [versions 'you sell'] to thy* **own people, or from the hand of** *thy* **own people 'buyest",** *do not oppress each other.*

15. **By the number of years after the Jubilee** *shalt thou from thine* **own people buy, and by the number of years of productivity shall he sell it** *to thee.*

16. **In view of the higher number of years after the Jubilee** *shalt thou* **a higher purchase-price, and in view of the lower number of years** *shalt thou* **a lower purchase-price measure; because it is the number of harvests he is selling** *to thee.*

IV. Divine Authority and Bounty

17. *Ye shall not each one oppress his own people, but stand in fear of your God.* **For I,** YHWH **am your God.**

18. And ye shall observe my decrees and keep my decisions and do them; then will ye dwell secure in the Land.

19. Then will the Land give its fruit, and ye will eat your fill and dwell securely in it.

20. And if ye say, "What are we to eat for the seventh year; we do not plant in it and cannot store up our produce ?"

21. For that case I bestow upon ye my blessing in the sixth year, such that it brings produce enough for three years.

22. Ye sow in the eighth year and eat from the existing produce until the ninth year; till the harvest comes in, ye eat the old.

V. Land-Release

23. But the Land shall not be sold definitively; because mine is the Land, and ye are tenants and migrant-workers with me.

24. In the whole Land which is your possession shall ye grant release for the Land.

25. *When thy brother falls into misfortunes* **and sells off some of his property, then a repurchaser comes for him, whoever is nearest related to him, and buys back what his brother had sold.**

26. And if no repurchaser is available, but he himself makes such a success of working the land that he himself is in a position to make the repurchase,

27. then he counts the number of years since he had sold it, and pays the remainder of the purchase-price to the buyer, then takes it back again into his own possession.

28. But if he has not produced enough to buy it back from him, then it remains in the buyer's possession until the Jubilee year; then it is released in the Jubilee and he comes back again into his possession.

VI. City-property

29. And if one sells a house in a walled city, there can be a repurchase of it until the end of the year; within those days is repurchase.

30. And if he does not repurchase up to filling for it an entire year, then stands the house which is in a city having [Hebrew *l'* 'not'; versions *lw* 'for it'] walls, definitively for its buyer for its generations; it shall not go out in the Jubilee.

31. But houses of villages having no enclosure-wall, to the field of the land shall it [versions 'they'] be reckoned; it shall have repurchase, or shall go out in the Jubilee.

32.   *But the cities of the Levites, houses of the cities of their inheritance, repurchase forever shall be for the Levites.*

33.   *And whoever redeems ['not' only Vulgate] among the Levites then the purchase of the house [H 'and'; G 'of'] the city shall go out in the Jubilee; because the houses of the cities of the Levites are their inheritance among the children of Israel.*

34. *Also pasture-land of their cities shall not be sold, for it is a permanent possession for them.*

VII. Usury forbidden

35. *And if thy brother beside thee falters and his hand trembles at your side, then uphold him, so that [GV + 'like'; or omit H 'tenant and migrant'] he may keep alive with thee.*

36. *Do not take from him usury or increase and fear before thy God, so that thy brother may stay alive beside thee.*

37. *Thy money shalt thou not give to him at usury, and at increase shalt thou not give to him thy food.*

38. I am YHWH your God, who brought you out of the land of Egypt to give you the land of Canaan, to be Elohim for you.

VIII. Slavery sanctioned

39. *And if thy brother falters and he sells himself to thee, thou shalt not toil with him the toils of a toiler.*

40. *As a hired servant, as a tenant shall he be with thee; up to the Jubilee Year shall he serve thee.*

41. *Then shall he be free of thee, he himself and his children with him*, and return to his family and reenter into his paternal possession.

42. For they are my servants, whom I brought out from the land of Egypt; they shall not be sold, the sale of a servant.

43. *Thou shalt not rule over him with harshness but shalt fear thy God,*

44. *But thy slave and thy maid whom thou shalt have* from among the goyim which are around thee, from them ye shall acquire slave and maid,

45. and also from the sons of the settlers sojourning with ye, from them ye shall acquire and from their family which is with ye, those to whom they gave birth in your land and who will belong to your possession,

46. these ye shall bequeath to your sons after ye to inherit as a patrimony forever, 'with them shall ye toil' [not in G]; but with your own people, the children of Israel one just like another, *thou shalt not rule over him in harshness.*

IX. Debt-defaulter repurchase

47. *And if the hand of a settler or migrant with thee abound while thy brother grows poor beside him and is sold to a settler or migrant with thee* or to the offspring of the family of a settler,

48. *after he has been sold there shall be repurchase for him; one of his brothers shall buy him out;*

49. either his uncle or the son of his uncle shall buy him back, or from the 'rest/flesh' of the flesh of his family one shall buy him back; *or his own hand shall make it and he shall be bought out.*

50. *And he shall reckon with his buyer from the year of his being sold to him up to the year of the Jubilee*, and the money of his sale shall be in the number of years, as the days of a hired servant shall it be with him.

51. If there still be many among the years, according to them he shall return the purchase price from the price of his sale.

52. And if little be left among the years till the year of the Jubilee, thus he shall reckon for him; according to his years he shall restore his purchase-price.

53. As a hired servant, year for year he shall be with him; he shall not order him about with harshness before your eyes.

54. *And if he is not thus repurchased, he shall go out in the year of the Jubilee, he and his children with him.*

55. For to me the children of Israel are servants; my servants are they, whom I brought out from the land of Egypt, I YHWH your God.

2. *Four other proposed source-divisions*

1. Here follows a simpler division presented as an appendix by Fager (*Land Tenure*: JSOT.S 153 p.123), with type-fonts intended to indicate directly the relative antiquity of the various portionS of the Leviticus 25 text.

> EARLIEST [(28b-31 large &) small caps]: laws regulating debt-sale;
> next (normal type): additions on repurchase and cities;
> **Early exilic redactor** (boldface): jubilee; some law-theology;
> *Later exilic priests* (italic): (fallow) additions to above;
> [Later (postexilic) priests] (bracketed): Yom Kippur, 3-yr food: added.

We will not here give in full (as for Elliger above) Fager's complete translation (of verses 8-55 only) in his respective fonts. Instead, we judge it more useful to give only a brief (7-verse) sample, as is customary in critical research, together with discussion of his norms not only in relation to the others here studied, but especially in regard to our very notion of this type of inquiry as "source-dissection".

The classic *Quellenscheidung* claimed to find in the Pentateuch as a whole four separate long continuous narratives ("J, E, P, and D") giving the whole of history through Moses (or Joshua: some spoke of Hexateuch or even Octateuch). Through the past century these four "strands" continued to be acknowledged: though J was varyingly divided in two, E lost many advocates, and (our) part of P became singled out as the "Holiness Code".

In comparison with this large-scale narrative maneuver, it would seem that we should not call our present "source recognition" a dissection at all. What we try to recognize, in very brief texts, is very brief *laws*, compared with other laws usually deemed earlier; then interpolated or *inserted in an altered form* into the single chapter we are studying. None the less, we find that this application of a "scaled-down" similar technique to a quite different body of materials may justly share the same name of "source-dissection".

We begin with verse 8, as Fager also does, but not in view of whatever motives may have moved him to do so. Our own aim here is rather twofold: first, these verses (though not all the earliest, indeed apart from interpolations, usually held to be the *latest*) contain the precise nucleus of the "Jubilee" which commonly gives a name and description to the whole of Leviticus 25; and secondly, as it happens, these verses embody all but one of the "meaningful" type-fonts chosen by Fager.

Leviticus 25, 8-14

(8) **You will count for yourself seven sabbaths of years, seven years seven times, so the length of the seven sabbaths of years will be 49 years.**
(9) **Then you will send about the sounding trumpet in the seventh month, on the tenth of the month,** [on Yom Kippur]. *You will send about a trumpet in all your land.*
(10) *You will consecrate the fiftieth year, and you will proclaim release in the land to all its inhabitants. It will be a jubilee for you. Each of you will return to his allotted land and each will return to his family.*
(11) *The fiftieth year will be a jubilee for you; you will not sow, and you will not reap what grows spontaneously, and you will not gather from the uncut vines.*
(12) *For it is a jubilee; it is holy to you. You will eat its produce from the field.*
(13) **In this year of the jubilee, each of you will return to his allotted land.**
(14) IF YOU SELL SOMETHING TO YOUR NEIGHBOR OR BUY FROM YOUR NEIGHBOR, EACH OF YOU WILL NOT WRONG HIS BROTHER.

It may be noticed at once that the reference to the Day of Atonement in verse 9 [brackets], specified by Fager as due to "later postexilic priests" is in the latest type-form. We may conclude that this link with penitence, prized

by some commentators, is seemingly regarded as (along with the three year￢
food shortage) the very last thing inserted into the whole chapter.

The properly jubilee-material, of which this citation chiefly consists, is
also indicated to be very late: chiefly from "later exilic priests" (verses 9b-12
in italics). These were doubtless supplementing the verses 8,9, and 13 (in
boldface type): "an early exilic redactor expanded upon the meaning of the
jubilee and added some theological warrant to the laws" (p.122).

The intriguing thing about this preceding paragraph is that Fager's own
analysis ("later" and "earlier" but not "earliest": including boldface verse 44)
has no occasion to mention the *very first emergence* of the Jubilee proper.
We are tempted to regard this as leaving a space open for my 1954 view of
an original Jubilee-proposal in the time of the Joshua-settlement, but
abandoned after the first try.

However, Fager's p.33 amid various references to my book seems to
maintain that we cannot seek any "original Jubilee text" because "the
beginnings of the written law lie in the casuistic regulations dealing with the
sale of landed property or of persons because of debt". To this is added an
Appendix finding no recourse to a Jubilee even in Nehemiah 5,1-13 and the
1 Mcb 6,49 fallow where it would be expected.

The final cited verse 14 must give us our clue to the "earliest" Jubilee
origins. It is in the type-font described as "uppercase letters": [this earliest]
"first level was a corpus of 'debt-sale laws', which regulated the redemption
or release of property or of persons who were sold because of debt". This
verse 14 is included in my above brief citation of the Jubilee nucleus also to
serve as a transition to one of the largest blocks of material which Fager
identifies in the chapter (verses 25-31 + 35-36 + 39-40 + 47-48b + 53; but
only the verses 28c-31 for an undisclosed reason seem to use barely-larger
capitals for the first letter of *all* words).

As a somewhat later supplement to these sections qualified as earliest,
are those given in "ordinary type" (not occurring in our sample above): "The
debt-sale laws were augmented slightly to expand upon those who could
serve as redeemers [parts of verses 47-49] and to exclude property within
walled cities [only Levitical: verses 32-34]. The verses 20-22 answering the
complaint about being short of food for three years are also in "ordinary"
type but in brackets, a late-late stage like the Atonement-Day noticed above.

A trifle which Fager and his readers will perhaps be glad to have called
to their attention is that some words seem to have dropped out of verse 16

on p.123: "**If there are many years, you will** [increase its price; if there are few years, you will] **decrease its price**."

All in all, the main thing we noticed in Fager's divisions is that three of the five parts are very late [(post-)exilic]. while the other two are "very early" (but without specifying their time relation either to each other or to Ex/Deut); no "earliest" except as explained above.

----

2. Among other proposed norms for source-division, a most original and enticing one is that of Cortese. The Jubilee-edict had a double goal in mind: the obvious one, to give hope and an end to propertiless debt-servitude; and an equally important one drawn from the *d^{e}rôr* of Isaiah 61,1.

The fixing of the terminal date at 50 years was a "ridiculous and cruel" length for the individual humanitarian goals envisaged[5]. But also humanitarian in a different way was the restoration of the whole land to the *whole* people by the termination of the exile, which is Second-Isaiah's concern[6]. And in this perspective the whole Jubilee law must have been inserted during the Exile but before its end, for which a total of 50 years was quite plausible.

Cortese supports this dating by a rapid vocabulary survey. In Lev 25 there are ten terms which he shows to be "neither preexilic nor postexilic". This survey might have been made more convincing by taking into account: first, that the fragments of very ancient usages which like most experts he finds salvaged in Lev 25 may be presented in the very words of their ancient formulation; and secondly, that at *any* stage the recompiler probably replaced some archaic words and possibly even some others with the then more current expressions. But these vocabulary-data may be a help to accepting a principal dating-criterion from Isaiah.

---

[5] Enzo CORTESE, "L'anno giubilare: profezia della restaurazione ? (Studio su *Lev*.25)", *RivBItal* 18 (1970; 395-409) 403. His vocabulary-study aimed p.401 to show the unity of the chapter must refer to the unity of its compiler (also p.398). who he admits used old materials. He analyzes also as unsupportive Rudolf KILIAN, *Literarkritische und formgeschichtliche Untersuchung des Heiligkeitsgesetzes* (kath. Diss. Tübingen 1969): BonnerBB 19 (Bonn 1963, Hanstein) 130-148, "Leviticus 25. Die Schichten".

[6] Walther ZIMMERLI, "Das 'Gnadenjahr des Herrn'" [< Fest. K. GALLING, *Archäologie und Altes Testament* 1970] in his *Studien zur alttestamentlichen Theologie*, Ges.Aufs.2. Theol. Bücherei 51 (München 1971, Kaiser) 222-234. Cortese claims support from Pierre GRELOT, "Soixante-dix semaines d'années", *Biblica* 50 (1969; 169-179), comparing Daniel 9 (7x70=500) years to the (round) 70 years in Jer 28-29 & 35 (p.172) and in Isa 61 with cognates in Lev 25,10 and its implicit allusion in Ezek 46,17 (p.179). See further A. LACOCQUE, *The Book of Daniel* (Nashville 1979, Knox) p. 178.

Another research by Cortese relates to the source-dissection of Lev 25 as part of "H". He holds that the earlier parts of H falsely follow Deut, but the later parts preserve better the distinction between *da'at* and *tôrah*[7].

3. Kilian's complicated analysis as presented by "hostile witness" Cortese can give us a hepful summary.   Kilian takes the non-universal fallow of Exodus 23,10 and debt/slave-release of Deut 15 as basis of the sabbath-year (and therefore jubilee) of Lev 25, "thereby destroying every possibility of the chapter's unity, which [Cortese] is trying to focus". But Kilian justifies the unity of compiler by the broader view that the *same* H-redactor who left out poor-aid in the Lev 25 sabbath year (and consequently jubilee), later includes from earlier material what is said to help the poor in the slave-release and *g'ullâ* laws.

Cortese protests that in making *only* the jubilee postexilic Kilian (*a*) has no support in other commentators who make the whole chapter postexilic, and (*b*) is constrained to all sorts of stylistic imitations of the exilic or earlier author of the law.   Undoubtedly we are dealing here with the thorniest interpretation-problem of the whole chapter, how to transform a varying-year fallow or debt/slave release into the universal fallow of the Lev 25 sabbath year and jubilee.   But whether Kilian has succeeded in this (or wanted to) or not, it would seem that Cortese must and does recognize that whomever he calls the "author" is in fact the (final) "compiler", and as such may well have gone the limit in introducing modifications to make the whole text consistent.

4. Cholewiński's 1976 *Heiligkeitsgesetz* (p.64, ftn.12 above) gives not only a compact redaction-criticism of Lev 25 but also separately a detailed comparison of it to the Deut 15 Shemittah.   He seems to agree with Elliger that shift between 3d sg., 2d sg. and 2d pl. is a valid source criterion.   On this basis (and also in view of "inclusions"): Group 1: verses 25b-31 (sale-valuation; walled cities) and 48-53 (Israelite slave of alien).   Group 2: contains fragments of the jubilee and fallow and most of 35-53 on slaves: held to constitute a logical and complete sequence.   Group 3, "showing only externally the 2d or 3d pl.": frame-verses revised by the second-group's author. He gives five sigla applying to the following verses: Vorlage 25-31.48-54; H5: 3-5.13-17.25a.35-46; HG: 1-12.17b-19.(23-55); Hd: 20-22; He: 32-34.

---

[7] Enzo CORTESE, "L'esegesi di H (Lev 17-26)", *Rivista Biblica Italiana* 29 (1981) 129-146. -- Rudolf KILIAN, *Literarkritische und formgeschichtliche Untersuchung des Heiligkeitsgesetzes*: BonnerBB 19 (1963), p. 130-148, Lev 25, Die Schichten.

Only on his p. 336 he defends his Lev 23,23.38.55 as H borrowings from Pg against the common view putting Hg *between* Deut and P; it would be hard to speak of a "common view" today; but as against Cortese I would defend a P largely existing before H but not excluding P(R)-corrections in H. Moreover Cholewiński's claim on p. 115 that an earlier H contained the sabbath-year law which was only by a later H worked into his Jubilee is probably not irreconcilable with some "common-view" P(R) additions still later. For his comments on debt-"slavery" and gage see p.64 above.

4. The "incidentally usable" in source-discovery efforts

Hardly anyone would accept *in globo* any one of these recent contributions to source dissection. But everyone will recognize that these five, as well as the several outdated analyses on which they are partly based, offer valuable facts and insights, which though hard to combine into a single coherent thesis, merit being kept constantly in mind.

If we were to attempt here to draw out only their indispensably valid claims, and replace the rest with almost-convincing claims from the others or new claims where necessary, we would simply be creating just one more in the long line of source-dissections with their merits and defects. Instead, therefore, using a kind of "canonical criticism", we will take the text as it stands and assume that it incorporates or adapts various earlier materials, for which a date or context can be only vaguely or cautiously assigned.

The text "as it stands" is in the final compilation of the Pentateuch, fairly commonly assigned to the Ezra-era. But that scribal era in fact contains two phases: one presumed to have been busied with the task or even to have brought it to completion during the Exile, another after the return to Judah (where in fact our Pentateuch may have been meanwhile almost completely known!) as described in Ezra 7-10 plus Neh 8 (and indeterminately more).

It would seem indispensable to qualify here "the text as it stands" with Blum's proposals as utilized by Albertz[8]. Blum claims to deny the existence of the sources JEPD, but in fact he replaces them with a K(omposition)^P and a K^D -- both drastically revised *after* the exile, in such a way as to include

---

[8]　Erhard BLUM, *Studien zur Komposition des Pentateuch* (1988 Heidelberg dissertation): BZAW 189 (Berlin 1990, de Gruyter); ch. 3, "Die Komposition der jüdischen Tora und die persische Politik", p. 333-360; Rainer ALBERTZ, *A History of Israelite Religion in the Old Testament Period, 2. From the Exile to the Maccabees* [Göttingen 1992]. tr. John BOWDEN (London 1994, SCM) ch. 5,3, "The struggle over the identity of the community" (pre-priestly/priestly K) p. 464-493. Now E. NICHOLSON, *Pentateuch in 20th century*, 1998.

with D most of JE (but with P Gen 1-11). In what follows, therefore, when the sigla P and D occur, they are to be understood as a convenience, referring to a widely-known hypothetical reality (now including Blum's reformulation) without rejection or acceptance, but with open-minded interest.

The "revisions" are presented by Blum in four stages closely linked to the Persian overlordship claims. D was revised with lay-orientation in view of being acceptable, first within the Judah community as its Pentateuch, and then eventually to the Persians as their approved "Constitution" by which Judah was to be governed.

Simultaneously P was being revised with cultic-priestly privileges in mind, and in view of its own acceptance as that Pentateuch. In a third stage, the divergences between the D and P "Kompositions" had to be reconsidered and hammered into a form judged suitable by both lay and priestly factions in view of being presented with complete unanimity to the Persian authorities as the "Constitution". There was also a "fourth stage", one or several, because Blum disclaims as "definitive Pentateuch" his K^{D+P}, because later further insertions were made.

We turn now to Cortese's attractive proposal for remedying the "unrealistic and cruel" 50 years bringing an end to individual enslavements by subsuming them into an (H_2 or H^R or P^R) reformulation based on Isa 61 for the end of the exile. But supplementing Cortese we would suggest that this insertion "during the exile but before its end" (as a vague but genuinely-predictive "prophecy") could just as well have been added by the very last postexilic Judah-returnee compiler as a "prophecy post factum" maintaining the hallowed "50 years" as close enough to 70 to serve for the seventh-seven individual release as well. We do not mean to say we are *choosing* this postexilic date; only that it could be left open as a possibility compatible with the essential of Cortese's.

It must next be noted that the "very late date" (P^H as debated above) commonly assigned to the Jubilee chapter of Lev 25, and within it to the Jubilee itself, is very often put in relation to the claim that the scribes working on the Pentateuch *during* the exile aimed at making sure that the lands in Judah from which the exiles had been driven out would be restored to them upon their return. It would result that a "latest" (postexilic) date would be unlikely. To this we would say that such reasoning is not implausible, but would not take precedence over (late-postexilic) dating-factors more intrinsic to the text.

We may regard as generally admitted the view that fallow or debt-release in a seventh year *varying* in the individual cases are fragments copied from an *earlier* legislation or usage: sometimes without due concern to harmonize them with later claims or decisions that the release should be made universal throughout the land for all individual cases involved.

Also, it seems fairly widely agreed that rather generic ethical norms, like the prohibition of usury or the obligation of helping a neighbor in need, which are spelled out in some detail in Lev 25, are likely to be copied from sources earlier than observances which are very specific, chiefly like the Jubilee itself or the universal sabbath year.

In admitting this, we do not automatically retract what is said in our 1954 book p. 207 about the likelihood that the most probable *Sitz im Leben* of a theorizing edict for a far-off remote future like the Jubilee would be at the time of first settlement in a new ("promised") land. In fact we have been pleasantly surprised by the number of more recent studies which have admitted this view at least as one of several which should be taken into account. "Earlier" and "later" are quite relative, and the "jubilee generalizations" even if composed orally as the very last portions destined to appear someday in Lev 25 could have embodied traditions and usages also orally familiar.

It has recently been claimed that the earliest known cases of being committed to writing in Israel could not be much before 800. But whenever our Bible began to be the object of scribal activity, this undoubtedly consisted in writing down existing traditions; and to the very end the scribal corrections and homogenizations were carried out on topics which had been familiar long before. None the less, we may admit here a certain force in recent researches into scribal activity in the Ezra era which had not been available in 1950, as we recently described in the final chapter of our Analecta Biblica 142.

And we may or must also admit that the exclusive interest of the pre-Jubilee decrees was in the ("slave", i.e. deeply indebted) small independent farmer. The wholesale adaptation of these decrees to a simultaneous recuperation of all alienated landholdings seems more suited to a (perhaps still awaited but proximate) return from exile with the intention of reclaiming all at once from their interim holders the lands of their previous possessors.

5. *Conclusions*

Our own new translation of Lev 25 from the Hebrew is given entirely in the type-fonts indicating the eight sources distinguished by Elliger. It is followed, among others, by Fager's Lev 25,8-14 in his source-dissection indicated by only five separate fonts. But it should be noted that these "differences of dating of origin" are rather redactions or interpolations than "Sources" in the classic JEDP sense.

In fact the whole of Ex 21 to Num 10 is a strung-together legal code only loosely connected to "P" into which it is inserted. As a subdivision of P has been generally admitted a distinct sub-source "H", the Holiness-Code Lev 17-26, which thus includes the Jubilee chapter. However, controversies have arisen as to whether to divide the original H from H-Redactor (as in Elliger) and also whether the part which includes Lev 25 is earlier or later than either the "true P" or the latest "P-Redactor".

Though most of these disputes presume a very late (or post-) exilic dating of (the final form of the) Jubilee-innovation itself and the organizational framework which it entailed, it is nevertheless generally admitted that some of the decrees in the rest of the chapter were much earlier traditions in actual use. This is true especially for the parallels in Ex 21-23 and Deut 15 & 23, though there are marked differences in formulation of these between themselves and as revised for Lev 25. From these have been drawn significant but varying sociological or historical conclusions.

The Jubilee-paragraph itself is often presented tacitly as an invention out of the whole cloth by the first-and-final compiler. But commentators sometimes do not exclude that there could have been an earlier form of this tradition also, even as early as the "Joshua-era" settlement which would afford its likeliest *Sitz im Leben*.

Among other recent source-dissections particular attention is merited by Cortese's treatment of Lev 25,10 as really a double or "double-meaning" statement. Its real importance is as an allusion to or enunciation of Isaiah 61,1 (further cited by Jesus in Luke 4,18) foretelling an eschatological liberation from miseries after the very long time which "50 years" stands for. With this twinning, the other meaning of the verse proclaiming liberation for the "dispossessed" only after at most 50 years is not as "ridiculous and cruel" as it seems -- especially since *family* rather than individual entitlement is the real goal of the law.

The earlier sources or traditions detected behind the Jubilee-chapter releases would more likely have been aimed to help the individual after his own six or forty-nine years, so that he would not have to wait for a far-off period during which neither he nor very many others would get the promised help. The Leviticus 25 compiler, with a scribal "fidelity plus freedom" transforms these items into a magnificent universality. But he utilizes the earlier formulas as widely as possible, as his own and as his own period's way of retaining continuity with essential religious origins.

On the other hand, it is now widely or universally agreed that the aim of the late-exilic compiler was to afford a basis for demanding restoration to the returning exiles of lands which their families had had to leave behind in Judah. This can easily be seen as a blessing for the (clan-) family, even if not so clearly for the individual who had to be made the proximate instrument of the "liberation".

ix

Historicity

The opening of Lev 25,1 "YHWH said to Moses on Mt. Sinai" is an "apparently historical" statement. It is repeated virtually identical at the end of Lev 26,46. "Historicity" is not a very popular word in most of today's researches of any Bible passage, and preference is often given to "the compiler's perspective".

1. Historicity and rhetoric intermingled

Hartley's Word Commentary holds that "God's word on Sinai" makes an *inclusio* for the whole of Lev 25-26 [seeming to add that this introductory formula occurs only here in Lev], but at once queries whether Lev 26,46 is a conclusion only for H 17-26, or for 8-26 or 1-26 (he does not ask whether only for Lev 25-26 as *inclusio* would imply, though only 26,35 is relevant to Lev 25)[1]. Thus this high-sounding statement is ultimateley relevant to rhetorical analysis rather than to historicity.

Elliger's more ponderous commentary p.243 says Lev 25,1 is from "Ph[1]" (principal compiler of the Heiligkeitsgesetz) and may well have been the *original* opening of H! His subdivisions for the sabbath year and jubilee sections are based mostly on *Numeruswechsel* (which we have examined very thoroughly in our ch.8); and his p. 349 says Lev 25,1 "sets the law strictly into the historical situation, namely to take effect (*inkrafttreten*) only at a time when Israel will be settled in the land which God will give it".

In this opening verse there are really two separate questions of (rhetorical) historicity: first whether God really said on Sinai *everything*

---

[1] John E. HARTLEY, *Leviticus*: Word Biblical Commentary 4 (Dallas 1992, Word) p. 418. -- Benjamin D. SOMMER, "Revelation at Sinai in the Hebrew Bible and in Jewish Theology", *Journal of Religion* 79 (1999) 422-451.

which follows, or only up to verse 23, which forms a kind of conclusion of
its own for (sabbath year and) jubilee; or only through Lev 25, or to the end
of the inclusio.

Regarding the more fundamental(ist) question, "Did God really speak
exactly these words to Moses ?", we would give the answer of most
believing exegetes today, "The historical religion of Israel is wholly based on
the conviction of a certain Moses, that God's will was communicated to him
and put by him into the Pentateuchal codes; and the scribes who eventually
wrote them down or copied them felt that they were remaining faithful in
introducing into the text small explanatory or updating notes."

2. Four distinct possibilities regarding historicity

Most commentators are concerned with a quite different kind of
historicity, involving really four separate questions:

(1) Were the jubilee laws ever (somewhere, somehow) seriously *decreed
for observance* ? It is fairly generally agreed (often except for the Jubilee
itself) that most of the provisions of Lev 25 were or reflect "very ancient
traditions". These in their time may have been regarded as "currently
prevalent and desirable practices" rather than as laws in a later juristic sense.
But this would be sufficient for considering them as "traditions which were
really and historically intended to be observed".

(2) Were the laws of Lev 25 (including the Jubilee itself), as decreed,
ever actually and regularly observed ? If there is evidence for this in some
cases, it proves also the historicity of the *decree*. If not, it still leaves open
the question of whether a given law was, as a fact of history, seriously
intended; but for various reasons just fell into abeyance.

(3) Were the laws feasible and actually intended for observance at least
one single time: likeliest the fiftieth year after the Exodus-style settlement,
or even after a Mendenhall-Gottwald "peasant uprising" origin of statehood.
The observance of these laws was partly scheduled to be observed only after
a very long time: in the case of the Jubilee itself a whole lifetime for most
of the persons involved. After so long an interval, laws like these, and
especially the Jubilee itself, would be subject to review.

Even if deemed unworkable at the moment of compiling, such laws
could be retained in the legal corpus as a past and possibly someday again
workable ideal (as in the Jesuit constitutions through many reworkings,
"never close the door while someone else is in the room").

This was my published view regarding the fiftieth-year Jubilee, recently
accepted by some few or noted as worth considering.

(4) Was the jubilee-organization of various ancient *observed* social-reform fragments only a visionary hope ? This would not necessarily mean that it was unrealistic or unworkable.

But a serious problem would be involved in the fact that the solemn cultic and cyclic aspects of Lev 25 required reducing to a single universal event practices of aid for the poor and "enslaved" originally intended to recur at seven-year intervals for the unfortunates concerned.

However, the simultaneity introduced into Lev 25 favors the increasing number of scholars who see it as a device for regaining the properties in Judah which had been lost by the Exile. This interpretation may be seen as an aspect of the now common claim that biblical historicity applies proximately and likeliest to the historical data surrounding the final compilation of the material.

Nevertheless, others still call the Jubilee chapter frankly an eschatological prediction (Isa 61, Lk 4), or even a mere inconsistent Utopian theoretical dream of hope.

3. *Some past or current views of Jubilee (-chapter) historicity*

Under the subtitle "authorship and origin", Hartley's Word Commentary p. xxxv really gives the more modernly usable part of the next subtitle, "The History of the Exposition of Leviticus" (by William Larchin p. xliii-xvi). If we skip such worthies as Philo, Origen, Rashi, and Calvin, we find that Hartley records the following positions:

(a) The conservative defenders of Mosaic authorship such as W. Gispen, Jewish M. Segal (with re-shapings), and Wenham's 1979 summary p.8. Here are some of the reasons given by Hartley for frankly accepting this view: The text frequently says "YHWH spoke these words to Moses"; the Levitical ritual suits the wilderness wanderings but not the postexilic marriage-law problems of Nehemiah; Ezekiel quotes Leviticus as canonical.

(b) Wellhausen's JEPD: For a century now Lev 25 has been loosely assigned to P by its defenders. Hartley now questions "whether P ever stood on its own" or were the priestly traditions woven into J and E[2]. He also stresses the fact that around the Holiness Code (Lev 17-26) and less-perceptibly also Lev 1-7; 11-15 has arisen a separate identity, hitherto still

---

[2]   Frank M.CROSS jr., *Canaanite Myth and Hebrew Epic* (Cambridge 1973), p. 324.

loosely connected with P.

Recently some have made an important issue of the claim that H (including Lev 25) was earlier than P. Others to save the last-minute character of the Jubilee itself admit that H may have been inserted before most of P, but that a final P-redactor may still have made some additions. Against the posteriority of P, Hartley even suggests that D (Deut 15 parallels to the release-laws!) may be later, citing Kaufmann (*Religion of Israel* 1956 p. 206): "In every detail, P betrays its [pre-D] antiquity".

(c) Chiefly a 1959 work of Koch ending with Lev 16 is cited for an outlook on modifications required for P (Gunkel, von Rad, Rendtorff)[3]. But Hartley wisely concludes "these studies have raised many questions for which solid, conclusive answers are hard to obtain". To these may doubtless be added those of Blum and Albertz treated on p. 96 above; and the more radical queries of the possibility of *any* "History of Israel" p.107 below.

(d) Like most scholarly defenders of the conservative position "God really spoke to Moses", Hartley recognizes with the critics some "seams" that have crept in: "the text bears the scars of a long history of transmission"; some laws were not worked well into their context; the Israelite community did some amplification ("needed", says Noordtzij). None of the cited examples concern Lev 25, but at the bottom of p. xlii it is noted that the repurchase laws had to be reformulated in view of the growth of cities; "an example of the subtle filling out and adjusting of the text during its transmission is seen in the textual tradition to which the Septuagint belongs".

Neufeld's rather brief survey of *šemittâ/yôbel* itself concludes: "*yôbel* is a fusion of very ancient ideas with new rules" somewhat inconsistent and exaggeratedly religious. But he then devotes six times as many pages to a survey of (largely Greco-Roman) data hinting that in Israel from 1200 to 600 efforts were being made to *revive* those ancient practices (among which he

---

[3] HARTLEY Lev. comm. p. xxxix; Klaus KOCH, *Die Priesterschrift von Exodus 25 bis Leviticus 16. Eine überlieferungsgeschichtliche und literarkritische Untersuchung*: FRLANT 71 (Göttingen 1959, Vandenhoeck & Ruprecht) p. 97-104; Gerhard VON RAD, *The Problem of the Hexateuch and Other Essays*, tr, E. DICKEN (New York 1966, McGraw-Hill); Rolf RENDTORFF, *The Old Testament; an Introduction*, tr. J. BOWDEN (Philadelphia 1986, Fortress) p. 161, & *The Problem of the Process of Transmission in the Pentateuch* (< BZAW 147, 1977) tr. John J. SCULLION: JSOT supp. 89. Sheffield 1990.

sees a "suggestion" that these prehistorically included periodic re-allotment of farm-lands, not perceptible among the biblical-era data), in the more orderly and religious, but bookish, form of our Jubilee[4]. Such a "reviving" or effort towards it would imply that the practices were historical to start with, except doubtless for the Jubilee forcing them into a procrustean unity.

4. Recent turmoil over whether and how any "History of Israel" is possible

The various decrees relevant to the Jubilee chapter are not from any historical narratives but from three law codes bearing only a loose relation to the parts of the Pentateuch in which they are lodged, or to some few episodes in Kings or Nehemiah. Nevertheless the decrees are in fact discussed -- indeed it is almost impossible to avoid discussing them -- in relation to various stages of what has until now been confidently called "the history of Israel".

For centuries it has been recognized that there are inconsistencies in the biblical history, which is the only one we had. These were treated as problems, and solved in various ways, or frankly admitted insoluble. Even the exegetical revolution of the JEPD-sources continued to produce histories more confidently than ever, "since now we know whether it is J's history or P's or whose that we are talking about."

But with the nineteenth-century outburst of biblical archeology this scenario changed radically. First of all we had voluminous written documents of Mesopotamian and Egyptian kings, more or less parallel to biblical history in their approach: and sometimes even mentioning by name (or with verifiably greater accuracy) biblical personages or events. Negligibly few of these materials were found in the territory of Canaan or Palestine.

Nevertheless numerous huge excavations were undertaken in Palestine. Though the main things discovered were decrepit buildings and mostly-broken pottery, these were cleverly utilized to reveal occupation-datings corresponding to the twenty-some main periods of biblical history.

Moreover a very informative and useful background was provided for many important biblical data not claimed to be in themselves "proved" or verified. The Baltimore archeologist Albright became a world-leader in recognizing and promoting such biblical relevancies: chiefly by his periodicals *BASOR* and *Biblical Archaeologist*, and by his students who soon

---

[4] Edward NEUFELD, "Socio-economic Background of Yōbēl and Šᵉmittā", *Rivista degli Studi Orientali* (held over from G. FURLANI Festschrift 32) 33 (1958; 53-124) p. 67; 71; 117.

occupied all the most influential University chairs.

What were the effects of this archeological revolution on the writing of biblical history ?

1) The most immediate effect was to *incorporate* these discoveries into any biblical history then perforce being rewritten. At first they were put in merely as illustrative or explanatory notes, and were highly appreciated even by the most conservative exegetes.

2) But quite soon the norm came to be "the historical data of the Bible are to be presented as true and valid *except* where proof of the contrary is available from archeology". This was much more of a challenge, not only to believers, but also to other scholars claiming that the invalidation of *some* biblical data shed a dubious reliability on all the rest.

The more conservative reacted by pointing out, rightly, that the archeological data were not *facts* in black and white to be accepted without murmur as more reliable than the Word of God. The archeological "facts" were indeed virtually all *interpretations*, almost immediately queried or denied by secular as well as religious experts.

However, a moderate course adopted in the Israel histories by Noth or Bright, or the Jerusalem Dominican Roland de Vaux in his *Institutions* (English title *Ancient Israel*) resulted in a certain widespread acceptance.

3) Not next in order of time, but eventually, some very few claimed that what we needed was a "History of Canaan" or a "History of Palestine" which like the comparable histories of Mesopotamia or Egypt would use *only* excavated data (though the long documents in cuneiform or hieroglyphic often contained errors as gross as any ever attributed to the Bible)[5].

So far this challenge has been met with the reply that for Canaan / Palestine the excavated material is far from adequate to the need; and anyway where written histories, even frequently erroneous like Herodotus, were available, they have always been used to piece out data from excavations or other sources judged reliable but inadequate. Thus it is reasonably asked

---

[5]   Keith W. WHITELAM, *The Invention of Ancient Israel; the Silencing of Palestinian History*. London 1996, Routledge; & "Between History and Literature: the Social Production of Israel's Traditions of Origin", *JSOT* (1991,2) 60-74: supported against Provan by most of the "twenty invited specialists", Dublin 1996) in Lester L. GRABBE, ed., *Can a History of Israel be Written ?* (Dublin 1996 meeting of 20 invited scholars): JSOT supp. 245. Sheffield 1997.

why is it less tolerable to use the Bible just like Herodotus where no other needed data are recorded ?

4) Meanwhile the fair-sounding norm "biblical history is utilizable except where it has been proved wrong" had been extended far beyond its original intention.   Thanks to the energetic iconoclasm, first perhaps of Lemche (whose numerous other writings on the Jubilee have been respectfully cited in this volume), then of Thompson and others, many experts had got to a point where a "History of Israel" could begin only with the Kings, perhaps even without David or Solomon, or Judah at all, only Samaria[6].

Not only the "History of Creation" but the whole patriarchal history of Genesis and the whole of Exodus were thus dismissed as unreliable or at best only limitedly historical legends. A similar caution has been shown even by those believers who have ventured to write a "History of Israel" at all.

5) Not necessarily linked, but perhaps congenial to the dim view of an (at most partial) Exodus or an Abraham were the varying Mendenhall and Gottwald proposals of the "origins of Israel" as an uprising of peasants within Canaan, perhaps part of or similar to the Ḥabiru revolts recorded at Amarna. In fact exegesis had already become tolerant to the notion of a gradual (questionably "seminomadic") infiltration, peaceful according to the European view (Alt/Noth), but by Albright linked with the (later queried) violent destruction of archeological sites in Canaan after 1200.

6) Meanwhile believers had continued industriously to interpret the Exodus and earlier traditions for the theological content which had been after all the main purpose of their origin. "Historicity" meanwhile, with a certain justification, had come to be taken as referring chiefly to the moment of *final* (Childs-style ?) compilation of the text, rather than to the moment at which the events are described as having taken place.

This can be called the "perspective" of the compiler, which quite apart from his "intention" included perforce much of his own religious, political, and also current historical background. (In this volume we have insisted on

---

[6] Thomas L. THOMPSON, "The Joseph and Moses Narratives". in HAYES-MILLER, *Israelite and Judaean History* [*not* Miller-Hayes ftn. 9 below]. London 1977, SCM. P. 149-180 . 210-212; & *The Origin Tradition of Ancient Israel, I. The Literary Formation of Genesis and Exodus*: JSOT supp.55. Sheffield 1987; *The Bible in History; How Writers Create the Past*. New York 1999, Basic.

recognizing the applicability of this concept not only to the *final* compiler, but also though less retrievably to the earlier compilers or originators whom he was copying.)

Since traditionally and likeliest the final form of our Pentateuch is due to the late-and-post exilic scribes linked to Ezra, there has recently been an immense focus on that Persian era as source of the "proximate" historicity of the Jubilee-related decrees. Our present volume has thus been forced to admit a certain plausibility in the view that the Jubilee was promulgated as a measure for the returnees' regaining of the Judah farms from which they had been dispossessed.

7) This intense flurry of Ezra-era research has led to two of what may be called "last-minute" developments on historicity, though of course there will be others yet to come. First, the allegedly brand-new source-dissection of Blum and Albertz on p. 97 above (even if largely a relocating and historicizing of P and D, dividing between them much of JE), rests on a very interesting analysis of what must have been the returnee priests' and laity's mode of conforming to Persian government requirements at that historic moment.

Secondly, and far outdoing all the rest in disposing of the claims of historicity, is Philip Davies *In Search of Ancient Israel*. He boldly claims (in a proposal presented as "heuristic" but undisguisedly on the right track) that a large workforce of scribes was paid by the Persian overlords for writing a history "of Judah" in a specially slanted way. Namely, not only the relatively few "Babylonian returnees", but disruptive elements from Egypt and many other lands forcibly resettled here, would acquire from such a "history of their own land" a wholly artificial sense of national identity and unity, and thus be more easily governable. For such a "History of Judah" the scribes would have no source except a few scraps of "Israel" tradition: but their assigned task was not to copy or compile but create out of the whole cloth a "History of Israel" -- which from then on was the only "biblical history"[7].

There has of course been an outraged reaction of moderates or even mildly conservatives, not attaining great published support so far, even if

---

[7] Philip R. DAVIES, *In Search of "Ancient Israel"*: JSOT supplement 143, Sheffield 1992: Ch.6, "Who Wrote the Biblical Literature. and Where ?"; ch.7, "How Was the Biblical Literature Written, and Why ?"; p. 120 "an exercise in imagination whose purpose is purely heuristic."

doubtless reflecting a vast silent majority[8]. But Davies has become a spokesman for Thompson, Lemche, Garbini, and the more cautious Soggin, in advocating an "Israel without a history" in the glittering pages of *Biblical Archaeology Review* as well as more soberly academic journals -- including the influential *JSOT* supplements co-edited by Davies himself.

8) What position can a believing Christian take today ? We must put at an extreme left not only Davies but a long fringe of partial clingers. But we must also put at an unsafe extreme right not merely "confessed conservatives" like Hartley but all those who like Alt, Noth, and (Davies' *bête noire* misuser of archeology) Albright, held firmly to a Bible-based "History of Israel".

So what can we use now for a biblical history ? Not safe enough, doubtless, but our safest resource today is Miller-Hayes[9]. Though it appeared a decade before the most recent and forceful positions, it makes clear how hard it strives to attain a tenable middle stance recognizing the usefulness of the Bible and following it wherever possible. This unfortunately cannot include the Exodus or anything before it, except doubtless as unproved traditions "to be taken into account".

But even in the remaining "History of Israel" the Bible leaves us with many gaps or inconsistencies, which the authors have striven to replace by a more logical or consistent position: in other words, as they frankly admit, by guesswork. To this modest effort have come not only jeers from the left, but even from the center comes the judgment, "Guesswork is not history".

To go farther, either to the right or to the left, would in the present state of our knowledge seem to be impossible. Most Protestant and Jewish believers seem to take this as their base, without scruple. Catholics have so far tried to keep unanswerable questions from rising, or refer to "common views" without explicitly adopting them, while awaiting a "History of Israel" judged acceptable universally or at least in declarations of their authorities.

The imposing new Oxford history of "the biblical world", despite the twist of its title, is really just a "History of Israel" with expert essays which

---

[8] Iain W. PROVAN, "Ideologies, Literary and Critical: Reflections on Recent Writing on the History of Israel", *JBL* 114 (1995) 585-606; rejoinders there by THOMPSON and DAVIES p. 683-698-705. -- R.N. WHYBRAY, "What do we Know about Ancient Israel ?", *Expository Times* 108 (1996f) 71-74.

[9] J. Maxwell MILLER & John H. HAYES [*not* Hayes-Miller 1977, ftn. 6 above], *A History of Ancient Israel and Judah*. Philadelphia 1986, Westminster. -- Stephen B. REID, "Miller-Hayes as 'Normal Science'", *JSOT* 39 (1987) 41, amid six critiques p. 3-63 from 1986 meeting: moderate but "this will be the last of its kind".

had been undoubtedly in preparation before the crisis became acute. It shows no more and no less attention to Mesopotamia and other neighboring nations than similar biblical histories. Its editor says on p. ix that its focus is "Canaan, Israel, Judea, and Palestine"; he admits that [now that all the chapters are completed] "the study of history is itself in flux ... within the last decade .. a minimalist approach to ancient Israel discounts the Bible as a credible witness .. radical skepticism"[10].

5. A view of the historicity and sequence of the Leviticus 25 norms

Our own view of the historicity of the separate sections must inevitably be related to the dating-hints suggested in our examination of the various source-divisions on p. 96-98 above.

i) The oldest part of Lev 25 would seem to be the prohibition of usury (35-38: an ancient law in poetic form with several recognizable augments) and related measures, bridged by Lv 25,23 from the sabbath-jubilee part. Its content also involves mainly brotherly mercifulness to a suffering fellow-Israelite, a humane outlook which betrays no juristic complications and could well have existed historically in any era.

ii) "Fallow" is in principle an agricultural term, but in none of the three Codes is it so designated, or indicated to improve farming-procedures: least of all in Lev 25,2, where it is a universal-cyclic seventh year, and for the honor of YHWH, or just for merited repose of "the Land"; there is no mention at all of "the Poor" unless very remotely they are included among "alien residents" apparently connected with the owner's farming-assistants.

The fallow in Ex 23,11, on the contrary, is expressly and solely intended for "the Poor". Not even the owner's work-force are explicitly included as having to nourish themselves all year with the "spontaneous growth". There is no mention of any benefits to agriculture: not surprisingly if as Hopkins maintains it would have been useful for this only if every *second* year instead of every seventh: whence he (alone! so far) concludes that it was or could have been historically a purely cultic cycle of seventh-year fallows operative *alongside* an every-other-year agricultural cycle.

---

[10] Michael D. COOGAN, ed., *The Oxford History of the Biblical World* (13 authors; New York 1998, Oxford Univ. Press), p. ix; on the coverage of "tension between urban and rural settings" there claimed, see STAGER p.76n8.

Even in such a case, it is virtually necessary to refer the "seventh year" of the fallow not to all the land of the whole country at once, but to the farm of each individual farmer, or likelier still to single ones among his various plots of land. Only thus could it have been of any real use to "the Poor" in accord with its declared intention; or (slightly) to agriculture, whose primitive link with any kind of fallow can hardly be altogether excluded.

The Shemittah of Deut 15 has no mention of any fallow, but we are invited to consider it as a parallel, or even an improvement and therefore of later date: because verse 7-11 insists on helping "the Poor, who will always be around". Moreover its two social-justice decrees are indeed "for" the seventh year: but for its beginning in verse 12 on "slave"-release; and for its ending in verse 1 on debt-cancelation ("suspension").

We see in this no convincing reason for doubting that Ex 23,11 is the most primitive mention of the Lev 25,2 seventh-year fallow, and among the earliest traditions later combined into the Jubilee chapter. It is not clearly later than Lev 25,37, but may perhaps be considered such, as being more technical and less universally-humane.

iii) There is something primitive in "enslavement" especially of a fellow-clansman. By this criterion we would tend to class among the more ancient legal traditions those which touch upon the "Hebrew slave" or his "redemption, *gᵉullâ*". But decrees also of this kind occur in the various parallel (Ex/Deut) contexts, with alterations which are thought to give a clue to their respective antiquity.

It is quite widely or fairly generally accepted that the two separate cases of Deut 15 represent a correction or improvement on the cognate Exodus passages. But some few exegetes recently and forcefully maintain that what Deuteronomy is correcting is the Holiness-Code formulation (Lev 25) which they say preceded it.

Ex 21,3 is in the same "Covenant-Code" as Ex 23,11; and like it is referred to a "seventh year", furthermore with a fallow which is expressly stated to be, in general humane terms, "for the poor". Taking into account that both these "seventh year" laws would seem to be more practical and workable if not in a universal way, but applicable to the dating of the single cases involved, we may well feel that Ex 21,3 is an earlier stage of the law of "Hebrew-slave" release.

iv) Release of defaulting "enslaved" debtors is legislated also by the right of a wealthier relative to intervene and "buy out" the debt (*gô'ēl, gᵉ'ullâ,* Lev 25,47 only for debtors self-sold to aliens; occurring also in Ruth and elsewhere, but not in our Ex or Deut passages). Lev 25,25 is dealing with basically the same problem and *gô'el*-repurchase rights under the aspect of the farm which the defaulting debtor was forced to sell.

Since this last is included before the material on cities, we may regard it as the earlier form. Later would be the items on an Israelite sold to an alien, Lev 25,47-53, which seems a kind of supplement to the legitimacy of *buying* alien slaves[11]. Such a practice (Lev 25,39-46) may well seem rather late, after the immigrant Israelites had attained a fair degree of prosperity in the Kings era, though not as late as the Jubilee-itself insert of Lev 25,54.

(*v*) The last decree or pericope to be inserted, for which no earlier parallel is discovered in Ex, Deut, or elsewhere in the Bible, is widely or even commonly admitted to be the Jubilee itself. In view of its destined millennium-long importance, Lev 25,8-13, is stated surprisingly briefly: a couple of Hurrahs, a fallow for YHWH, and a homecoming.

But the homecoming involves the cancelation of a land-sale long ago, and in this regard are introduced immediately in Lev 25,14-17 picayune but important regulations which are now put forward as having governed that long-ago event in view of the now-present jubilee.

A chief factor inducing many to favor a latest-feasible date for Lev 25,8-13 itself is that it would thus be an invention or retrieval from the late-exilic period of Ezra, and thus really aimed to regain the property, not of any individual or family. but *en bloc* all the property of the returnees which was being utilized during the Exile by intruders.

Such a late date for the actual compilation of the Jubilee law would not exclude that it too, like most of the other items in the chapter, had been some sort of earlier tradition, such as precisely a Joshua-era settlement provision foreseen for 50 years later. But when that time finally rolled around it may have been considered impracticable, but not wholly forgotten as an oral tradition, though not written down in preserved pre-Ezra sources.

6. Conclusions

Historicity is not now prominent in biblical study as compared with more important aspects like theology and insight. It is even generally maintained that biblical narratives reveal to us something of the history of the period in

---

[11] Christiana VAN HOUTEN, *The Alien in Israelite Law*: JSOT supp. 107. Sheffield 1991 (p. 53n7 above).

which they were definitively compiled, rather than of any earlier more legendary period in which took place the events described. In any case the passages relevant to the Jubilee occur in three legal codes, connected indeed but only loosely with historical narrative in the Pentateuch ("P", or perhaps more properly some redaction of "H").

If we insist on asking, "Is Lev 25 or everything in the three codes réally historically 'God's word to Moses on Sinai'" ?, the answer is commonly admitted to be "Judeo-Christian religion is wholly based on the historical tradition of a conviction of Moses that God had somehow communicated to him a *Tora*, which was eventually written down by scribes; these at each recompilation felt that they were remaining faithful in introducing small notes of explanation or even alteration in accord with usages prevalent at their own date."

The Jubilee as a historical event is nowhere attested, though most of the other legal items in the chapter are. The Jubilee as a law really intended for observance is only vaguely attested in Lev 27,17; Num 36,4; Ezek 46,17; or by its alternative name *d^{e}rôr* (release, Lev 25,10) in Is 61,1 (Lk 4,19). Some hold that the only "historical event" of the Jubilee was the *proclamation* of a far-off eschatological well-being or liberation.

Cognate decrees within the jubilee chapter (fallow, debt-slave release) are strongly attested but with inconsistent formulation in Ex Deut. The fallow itself is nowhere linked with any likely agricultural origins, and as described especially in its simultaneous and essential relation to the Jubilee (but also if rotating only once every seven years) could possibly be historical only as a cultus (sometimes attested, at least as "reckoned", varyingly).

There are still defenders of Jubilee historicity as part of "Mosaic authorship" or even in indicated relations to "P" as in itself a history. Blum's intriguing reconstitution of P (also D; between them salvaging most of JE) favors the widely-held historicity of the Jubilee as an Ezra-era move toward restitution of Judah property to returnees. Exceptional and somewhat Greek in outlook is the emphasis on Lev 25's "reviving" of (therefore early historical) social-justice measures.

Nineteenth century archeology discovered long Mesopotamian and Egyptian documents illustrating and even rectifying biblical parallels. Twentieth-century Canaan-area excavation found almost no documents, but confidently used broken pottery and tumbled buildings to create a generally agreed chronology for the biblical occupation.

Exegetes at first regarded excavated materials as merely illustrating or clarifying the biblical narrative, but gradually admitted that "history can utilize the Bible only where excavation has not proved it wrong"; some even proposed that a "History of Canaan" as of Mesopotamia or Egypt must be written with no recourse to the Bible or any non-excavated document.

Even moderate acceptance of the Bible resulted in histories beginning only with or after the Exodus or even Jeroboam I, on the ground that largely legendary traditions had to be "doctored", even by amputation; or at best supplying the "gaps" by sensible "guesswork". But "history is not guesswork", and some more recently go so far as to claim that no "history" of biblical Israel can be written at all.

Without ignoring the admixture of truth in these recent outlooks on archeology and history, we feel securely within the competent majority in claiming that the Jubilee-decree itself was the last part of Lev 25 to be composed, near the end of the Exile and in view of repossessing Judah lands, though quite possibly retrieving a similar proposal from as early as the Joshua-settlement era.

There is merit also in the claim that verse 37 was the earliest part of the chapter to become part of Israel's ethic, because it is written in metric-proverbial form and though nominally treating only briefly interest on loans, actually is concerned with the most general humane norm of saving a fellow-human from "going under".

Assuming that the paragraphs about cities are likely to be late, and along with them the legitimating of Israelites' purchase of foreign slaves, we are left with a couple of fairly early and noteworthy references to a "seventh" year. Varying claims have been put forth to make Deut 15 either earlier than Ex 21 and 23, or even later than P (H).

But we still hold with the probable majority that the "fallow for the Poor" is earliest, doubtless rotating though not thereby saving any of the agricultural usefulness of its likely origins. From the earliest biblical mentions, however, it was fully cultic; no less than when it was "revised" to be universal as basis of the "seventh seven" Jubilee formulation.

x

N o w   2 0 0 0

It would seem appropriate to conclude with some reflections on the publications of this past half-century which have stressed chiefly the relevance of the Jubilee to the special requirements of the current day. Deserved welcome has been enjoyed by Cardinal Tettamanzi's 1999 *Anno di grazia, tempo di gioia. Meditazione cristiana sul Giubileo.* Other published insights include not merely the advances in Jewish and Christian confessional theology[1]. Equally to be kept prominent are the urgent obligations of the First World as well as the needs of a Third World in somehow adapting a sadly unbalanced global economy.

1. Proclaim a Jubilee: the Land is the Lord's

The cultic cyclic proclamation aspect of the Jubilee is far from absent in our 2000 jubilee proclaimed by the Pope and welcomed in various ways by other religions and secular authorities. The popes have in fact taken the initiative, ever since Boniface VIII in 1300, in proclaiming a "remission of debts" (chiefly of guilt, by indulgences), and later not merely for the centenary and millennial years, but for other intervening ones as well which were jubilees of specific non-centenary events.

Welten hints that Luther's change of the Latinizing *Jubeljahr,* to more properly Hebraic *Jobeljahr,* left his reform of Christianity without any Jubilee, and with him "indulgences" also have been pushed away from the

---

[1] We need not here recall our 1954 "Social Theology of the Jubilee". Its four points have been cooperatively summarized in Gordon J. WENHAM's 1979 *Leviticus* and again in Walter C. KAISER,Jr.,"Leviticus",*New Interpreter's Bible* 1 (Nashville 1994, Abingdon;985-1191)1174. Now L. DE CHIRICO,"Biblical Jubilee", *Evangelical Review of Theology* 23 (1999) 347-362.

focus[2]. But the papal and conciliar declarations themselves never tire of proclaiming that ours is *par excellence* the Ecumenical Age, and John Paul II has insisted that his fondest hope for the year 2000 has been that it will bring us, if not actually into, at least perceptibly closer to, the unity of the Christian Church[3].

A collection by Zappella begins as usual with scrutiny of Ancient Near East data; biblical defense of exilic origin along with history of even later Neh 5; and a survey of NT references especially involving *áphesis*. But quite unusually after that it presents the views especially of Origen and Chrysostom, also not overlooking Cyril, Theodoret, Hesychius and Eusebius: all of whom considered the Jubilee as a historical reality, but chiefly as a moral norm urging to give up as much as half one's property to the poor.

The book adds a collation of some sixty Christian Arab manuscripts from the (other) millennium. Five give Ibn Ṭayyib's very succinct and literal though curiously ordered contents of Lev 25. The other fifty-some are from A.D. 1150 Marqus Qunbar, evidently very popular despite his undeniably capricious religious biography, and an allegorism far surpassing Origen's. He begins Lev 25(,2) thus: "Christ our Redeemer was N° 7" [in the series Adam-Noah-Abraham-Moses-Prophets-Baptist]. The causes of poverty, intertwined with Adam's sin, Rom 7,19, and Mt 5,42, are then surveyed in OT-NT with bare allusion to Lev 25,20-22 before returning at the very end to the decree that in the seventh year the land was to rest[4].

These curious and largely unusable later-Christian citations are nevertheless very important as a warning to us that the Jubilee chapter has its own history of use within the whole duration of Christianity; and it would be highly desirable to dig up at least some further fragments of this history to piece out the background of Jubilee 2000 as a Christian proclamation.

---

[2] Peter WELTEN, "Erklärt dieses fünfigste Jahr für heilig. Entwurf und Wirklichkeit des Sabbatjahres", *BerlinerTZ* 8 (1991; 121-8) p. 126.

[3] Georges COTTIER, "Réflexions théologiques sur le Jubilé", *Seminarium* 39 (1999) 73-81 is largely devoted to the solution of dilemmas of the ecumenical dialogue.

[4] Marco ZAPPELLA, ed.(p. 7-10; 241-272) *Le origini degli anni giubilari. Dalle tavolette in cuneiforme dei Sumeri ai manoscritti arabi del Mille dopo Cristo.* Casale Monferrato 1998, Piemme. 1. Cristina SIMONETTI, Gli editti di remissione in Mesopotamia e nell'antica Siria, p. 11-73; bibliog. 71-3; 2. Francesco BIANCHI, Il Giubileo nei testi ebraici canonici e post-canonici, p.75-132 (sua datazione 113-9); bibliog. 133-7; 3. Georg SCHEUERMANN, Il Giubileo negli autori del Nuovo Testamento. p. 139-180; bibliog. p. 180-2; 4. Paola MADARO, Il Giubileo nell'interpretazione dei Padri Greci. p. 185-219; bibliog. 219-220; 5. Laura BOTTINI, Il Giubileo in due autori arabo-cristiani, p.221-238; bibliog. 238-9.

But the biblical roots and the very nature of this cultic proclamation inevitably point beyond itself to the social and economic life of the worshipers. I may be pardoned here for mentioning a remembrance of the eminent Dominican exegete Pierre Benoit. He was kindly guiding me on my first visit to Jerusalem, when a beggar accosted him. Without giving him anything, Benoit said something amiable to him, and the beggar showed signs of contentment. I asked what it was he had said in Arabic, and he told me *ya'tîk Allah,* "Allah will give to you". Neither of the two would have seen the least suspicion of cynicism in this reply; it gave quite suitable reassurance to both, and Père Benoit encouraged me to use it myself when occasion offered.

Doubtless there are involved here depths of Muslim *maktûb*-"fate" religiosity which most Christians do not share. But I could not help an initial reaction. A beggar, a whole hungry two-thirds world, asks us for help. We reply amiably, "Oh yes, fine! We will declare a Jubilee: 'The Land is the Lord's'". To a Western outlook it seems that something more active and socioeconomic is needed in the present crisis to make such a cultic answer sincere.

2. Relevance of Isaiah 61 and Luke 4

We took note of Cortese's proposal for bettering of our understanding of the Jubilee release as not merely from slavery after fifty long painful years. He finds that Isa 61,1 is used to give a simultaneous more important second and "eschatological" meaning to Lev 25,10[5].

Sloan has recently taken aim against the view of Yoder that what Jesus was actually proclaiming in the synagogue of Nazareth was a real universal jubilee in exactly the sense of Lev 25[6]. Sloan points out that since Jesus

---

[5] CORTESE above, p.94 n.5; and on Isa 61 ZIMMERLI there n.6; further James A. SANDERS, "From Isaiah 21 to Luke 4", in Morton SMITH Fest., *Christianity, Judaism, and Other Greco-Roman Cults,* ed. J. NEUSNER (Leiden 1975) vol. 1, p. 75-106.

[6] Robert B. SLOAN, Jr., *The Favorable Year of the Lord: a Study of Jubilary Theology in the Gospel of Luke* (diss. Basel; Atlanta 1977, Scholars), p. 10; 167 on Yoder, emphasizing the use of *áphesis* and its frequent varying NT senses. -- John H. YODER, *The Politics of Jesus* (Grand Rapids 1972, Eerdmans) p.36 and citing on p. 64 André TROCMÉ, *Jesus and the Nonviolent Revolution* (tr. Michael H. SHANK & Martin E. MILLER; Scottsdale PA 1973, Herald), p.41. -- August STROBEL, "Die Ausrufung des Jobeljahrs in der Nazarethpredigt Jesu. Zur apokalyptischen Tradition Lc 4$_{16-30}$", in Erich GRÄSSER, *al., Jesus in Nazareth*: BZNW 40. Berlin 1972. de Gruyter. P.38-50.

refers to the Jubilee *d^erôr* only via Isaiah 61, its prophetic-eschatological aspect dominates, as also in Daniel, *Jubilees* 1,21-25, Qumran 11Q Melchizedek, and Babylonian Talmud Sanhedrin 11.1 (97b).

We recognize the value and need of this emphasis on Jesus' own aims in his allusion to the Jubilee *d^erôr*. We may also wonder whether it was only by chance that in following Isaiah he omits specific reference to property-restitution, which really is the core of the Jubilee; and both make the "help for the poor" consist chiefly in preaching the Gospel to them.

Moreover between the Hebrew Isaiah's "liberty to captives" and "release to prisoners" Luke 4,18 inserts with the Septuagint "restoring sight to the blind" (not in MT). This may represent a scribal effort to recapture from the end of the Hebrew verse a rare or corrupt sense of *peqah* "release", elsewhere always from blindness; here with *qôah* (? "prison").

_____

It should not be overlooked that the jubilee renovation extends also to forgiveness and reconciliation with our enemies or moral debtors[7]. Doubtless for so lofty an ideal "the true year of Jubilee (completing the Atonement-Day) is yet to come"[8]. Meanwhile as a culmination of the Holiness Code, the Jubilee "legitimates and facilitates a program of individual ethic"[9].

Whatever may have been the precise implications of either Isaiah or Jesus in alluding to the Jubilee *d^eror*, it would seem that to most commentators on the Levitical Jubilee its relevance to our own day must consist chiefly in a more equal redistribution of property, by "cancelation of debts".

3. Post-Christian Liberation and Jubilee

Sharon Ringe in her key chapter on "Jubilee Traditions in Hebrew Scriptures" focuses chiefly the problem of a transit from recurrent seventh year or merely occasional measures to a solemn universality combining all those efforts at a more fair distribution of the Land's resources, and pointing with Isaiah 61 to a future perspective far beyond.

Advancing somewhat beyond the common approach, she begins by reducing all pre-Jubilee measures to the three existing Codes or legal corpora:

---

[7] Beat WEBER, "Vergeltung oder Vergebung ? Matthäus 18,21-25 auf dem Hintergrund des "Erlassjahres", *ThZ* 50 (1994) 125-151; also his *ZNW* 83 (1992) 161-182.

[8] Charles R. ERDMAN, *The Book of Leviticus, an exposition* (New York 1951, Revell), 133.

[9] Eckart OTTO, *Theologische Ethik des Alten Testaments*: ThWiss 3,2 (Stuttgart 1994) 249.

the Covenant Code (with its Hammurabi-cognate, which however has a more generous slave-term of only three years); the Deuteronomic Code with the reforms of 2Kgs 22-23 (Jer 34,8-22); and H, the Holiness Code of Lev 17-26 with all the more ancient usages subsumed into Lev 25.

In the Covenant Code, both Ex 21, 2-6 and Ex 23,10-11, she insists not only that both the poor-aid fallow and the slave-release were for *variable* years in accordance with the need, but also that "Hebrew (slave)" though ultimately meaning here just Israelite must have deeper nuances.

With the echoing of these two laws in Deut 15 she feels able to define "Hebrew" as the (ethnic-Israelite) legitimate holders of slaves both "Hebrew" and alien. From both sections of the law have disappeared references to the fallow and to aid of the "simple poor". The shemittah "cancelation" of debts as mere suspension for one year (though "after" seven years) would better fit Ex 21,1 (after six; Deut 15,4 foresees no poor left at all), though it would make for "tight credit", ill-compatible with continuance of the impoverished in Deut 15,7-11. She finds much to add to the actual functioning of Deut 15 in the $d^e r\hat{o}r$-decree of Zedekiah (Jer 34,8-22); Neh 5,13 less clearly relevant.

But with Lev 25 she gives voice to her most nagging preoccupation. "The legislation itself is unclear about whether the Jubilee was intended to be a repeated event or a single occurrence. Leviticus 25:15 implies a cyclic pattern of Jubilee years, [according to which] the value of the land is to be calculated. ... Elsewhere in the chapter, one looks forward to a jubilee that might indeed be a one-time redistribution of the land following the occupation [as North 1954] or perhaps more accurately, the return from exile. This ambiguity concerning the number of Jubilees may reflect ... both the cyclical sabbath-year laws and the royal decrees of release ... that appear to have occurred only once in the reign of any sovereign"[10].

She concludes only that "whatever the intent of these laws, they were not enacted as a part of public policy [but] bear witness to the continuing power of the image of God as sovereign [, its] ethical consequences ... and the Isa 61,1-2 (Lk 4,18-19) establishment of God's eschatological reign."

The Jubilee as a very early rather than postexilic Jewish legislation is seen as "restoration of all things", *apokatástasis pántōn* Acts 3,20[11].

---

[10] Sharon H. RINGE, *Jesus, Liberation, and the Biblical Jubilee*: OverturesBT 19. (Philadelphia 1985, Fortress) p.27, citing doubtless for the italic words R.W. KLEIN, *Israel in Exile: a Theological Interpretation*: OverturesBT 6 (Philadelphia 1979, Fortress) 90-96.

[11] Michael LANDMANN, *Messianische Metaphysik*: Jüdische Miniaturen 1 (Bonn 1982, Bouvier; "Schmitta und Jowel", p. 79-102) p. 101.

4. Some irrelevancies in Leviticus 25 for today's Jubilee

We are dealing in this chapter with the relevance of Lev 25 to our own day especially in matters of socio-economic reform and a better approach toward an always-remote egalitarianism. With this in mind, it is no longer of importance whether the Jubilee was intended as a mere hope and warning, or as a law that was intended to be really put into effect, at least once as a "trial run".

Nor is it of much importance in today's purview to discuss whether the seventh year for debt-slavery release and better access of the poor to the sources of supply, of which the Jubilee is ultimately a heightening, was intended to be universal all over the country or rather linked to the sixth/seventh year of individuals' "enslavement".

For one thing today we are no longer speaking, except justifiably in the synagogue, of a single relatively tiny "chosen people" with a small fringe occasionally involved in their enslavements. The message of the Jubilee for today, as our Jewish brethren would be the first to insist, is a proclamation of global unity in working to relieve economic unbalance.

Gnana Robinson writes, "A group of Asian theologians was dealing with the problems of the developing lands, especially the burdensome economic disparities between this world's developed and underdeveloped areas. One of them said, 'We must proclaim a Jubilee; the earth's riches must be fairly divided among its dwellers in accord with its basic needs, not for consumerism' ... Institutions arise in concrete situations, to satisfy certain societal needs and fulfil specific social, political, or religious duties. The Jubilee-Year, whether ever reduced to practice or not, was not some individual's artificial or idealistic invention [but] it could have been the invention of an individual or group in dire need .. in a crisis such as that of the return from Babylon"[12]. The article goes on to show its development in such circumstances, and concludes with the need of a similar international religious dynamism for today's crisis.

The above citation rightly suggests that the biblical Jubilee must remain first and foremost a cultic proclamation, an acknowledgment that "the Land

---

[12] Gnana ROBINSON, "Das Jobel-Jahr. Die Lösung einer sozial-ökonomischen Krise des Volkes Gottes", in Fest. K. KOCH, *Ernten, was man sät*, ed. D.DANIELS, *al.* (Neukirchen 1991; 471-494) p. 471; 476. P. 489 cites H.E. VON WALDOW, "Social Responsibility and Social Structure in Early Israel", *CBQ* 32 (1970; 182-204) p.189 "the religious character of the social laws in Israel is especially apparent from their comparison with Ancient Near East parallels".

is the Lord's". And "the Land" quite literally, with its minerals and forests (though one might quibble about sea and sky), means all sources of production helpful or needed for well-being, *human* well-being not selfishly but including proper human attitudes toward the whole of creation.

All this "belongs to the Lord", not arrogantly as if he were claiming the right to sit on it and exclude from it all the creatures who desperately need it; but rather because the Lord is the guarantor of adequate right of access for all to the source of supply which is what is meant by "the Land".

5. Role of the small farmer in the ancient jubilee

A graver hurdle must be overcome in attempting to adapt the time-bound wording of the Jubilee to the timeless demands of justice and decency which it unmistakably has behind it. The reader of these pages cannot have escaped noticing that what the Jubilee is all about is the trials and tribulations of the small independent farmer.

The passages on the threat of debt-slavery, without enumerating specifics, indicate clearly a plight due to sickness or weather and similar natural phenomena over which he has no control. Nothing is even hinted at his long hours of back-breaking toil, sometimes sixteen from dawn to dusk, also with his wife and even very small children at times of urgent harvest or threatening crisis. There is also (if we date the Jubilee formulation during the Monarchy) the burden of taxes.

This is a world virtually unknown to Europe and North America, where the thousands of pages of exegesis of the jubilee have come from. We know from romance and history that such situations existed until quite recent times. But the farming conditions in which the Jubilee took origins are apt to be dismissed alongside *Pithecanthropus erectus* with his club and his woman dragged by the hair, as a phase of prehistory no longer relevant to actual life.

Yet we know that this is far from the case. In the "two-thirds world", including most of Asia and Africa and much of Latin America, we are vaguely aware (from journalists, returning missioners, anthropologists) that most of the population eke out a painful and threatened existence on small farms, often as tenants of others scarcely better off than themselves. Elsewhere they are set to preparing and neatly packaging fish and meat or fruit-delicacies far too costly for their own nutriment but to be sold to epicures 5000 miles away. More recently, for a daily salary seeming princely by comparison, they work twelve hours in cramped rickety fire-hazards, assembling computer-parts to be sold in the West at 1000% profit.

———

Upon careful re-reading, it may well appear that the Jubilee laws are not really *concerned* for the failing small farmer; they are only *about* him. What they are really concerned for is maintaining small properties in the same family for all generations forever. In light of this aim, Cortese (p.116 & 94n5 above) would have to admit that the Jubilee's long long range solution was neither ridiculous nor cruel. Whether it would have worked, or really was intended to, it would have to be admitted suitable to the chief aim.

The family and its perpetuation has even recently been seen as a factor in the Jewish religious belief in afterlife. Starting from Mitchell Dahood's Ugaritic-based strivings to rediscover in the Old Testament a real expectation of life after death, Brichto maintains that in this purview "property was essentially a religious concept"[13].

In any case, for all its focusing "the family (and the economy)" rather than the individual, throughout the jubilee-chapter there inevitably shines through an elemental social justice and decency. The purpose of keeping the ownership of farmland divided into small plots within the family was to avoid latifundism, and that means to avoid precisely the situation which agonizes us today: a world or a nation where far too few have far too much, and millions starve.

But the focus on the small individual farmer's plight has also unmistakable overtones about justice and decency to him, even if this is not seen as requiring more prompt action than being put off to his death or even much later. Elderly people with even a small property to bequeath feel a certain dignity in taking measures so that it may be done properly. But if we are rightly evaluating the real agenda of the jubilee wording, we will have to look deeper to inquire how its spirit can prompt action for today.

———

In the worldwide recognition of need for improving the lot of "the poorest of the poor", it cannot be denied that Communism had a neat and logical solution, which in fact appealed preoccupyingly to some exponents of Liberation Theology. And for many decades it succeeded, even if at the cost of untold murders and cruelties, in making food and lodging and transport seem cheap even to the poorest.

But it unexpectedly crumbled in 1989, whether because of self-indulgence at the top as was horrifyingly publicized in Romania, or more

---

[13] Herbert C. BRICHTO, "Kin, Cult, Land and Afterlife -- a Biblical Complex", *HUCA* 44 (1973; 1-55) p.5.

likely because its contempt for the profit-motive was inadequate to harness general cooperation for the common good.

Sometimes we find or imagine a similar situation existing in "free" countries rich enough in natural resources, where the plight of the poor is thought of as due to public officials incurring enormous national debts of which a sizable share ends up in their own pockets, or in Swiss bank-accounts of tax-shirking wealthy citizens.

This possibility, or rather this obscurely-recognized existing reality, is often exaggerated by activists who are not in a position to do anything about it; graft in government may be more alarming in some countries than in others, but with the best will in the world it is hard to suppress completely.

On the other hand, the international coalitions like world banks and the World Trade Organization, though (even in their own interest) sincerely preoccupied with measures for diminishing the horrifying discrepancies between per capita wealth in the various parts of the world, nevertheless perforce see the poor world's problems in terms of their own.

An example would be the United States using its tremendous economic and political force to impose on the poorest countries of East Asia and elsewhere a prohibition of child labor and a minimum wage. Both these improvements would have an incidental advantage of diminishing competition with First World markets. But it is hard or impossible for prosperous nations to realize that the "almost nothing a day" for which these people work is in fact a few pennies to buy enough dry bread to keep from starvation. Similarly if the whole family from earliest childhood does not get out into the field from dawn to dusk to gather the crop, they will have no harvest.

Obviously exegetes are not economics experts; and we have to have confidence in those who are. They at least, in their exalted positions in multinational coalitions, know what these problems are: know only too well, so much so that when in all good will asked to provide a solution, sometimes can only wring their hands in despair.

This is the situation requiring an adaptation of the jubilee to 2000!

6. *Jubilee cancelation of debts*

To remedy the evils of third world destitution, a convenient and precisely-formulated phrase has been found in Deut 15,1 "the cancelation of debts" of poor nations, or the equivalent "cancelation of (debt-)slavery" in the Jubilee Lev 25,54. Thanks to influential recommendations of Pope John Paul II and demonstrations by lobbies in many wealthy western countries, coalitions of international banks and the International Monetary Fund have already announced their intention of canceling a notable part of the national debt of the poorest countries.

The governors of these coalitions will have undoubtedly considered and found satisfactory solutions to obstacles which may occur to the common man not well versed in economics or high finance. In the pages of exegesis the main problem which has been recognized and debated is whether there is a real "cancelation" or merely a one-year "suspension" (of ? interest). We will not renew that debate here, because it is obvious that those who advocate "cancelation of debts" as a needed measure of social reform are not talking about mere postponement of either interest or principal.

One present problem of the banking leaders is: where did the indebtedness money come from? It rarely or never happens that a single individual is so rich that he can lend, even at intervals, the whole national debt of a country even much smaller than Brazil. In such an unlikely case only, one would know *who* exactly is condoning the debt and what he personally is losing by this act. But the money for international loans virtually always comes from banks, and thus ultimately from *depositors* -- most of them big companies or quite wealthy depositors. It was doubtless easy for the coalition leaders to protect the few depositors who really need the income to live on.

Another question the debt-cancelers will have had to decide is how to face the charge of unfairness to other countries whose debt is almost as great but who have kept it down by zealously prosecuting tax-evaders and thus being able to pay promptly the interest and part of the principal,

———

A further dilemma for the bankers: Just how can debt-cancelation help the poorest of the poor, at the very bottom ? -- which is really the goal of the worldwide cry. Proximately, by improving the whole local economy, is the usual and somewhat Western-sounding answer (*sotto voce*: it would simultaneously benefit also the West by increasing export-markets).

For the needed improvements, perhaps there is illegally enough money in the hands of tax-evaders -- some of whom have been principal benefactors of hospitals, schools, and other pious works. But at best, the help which will trickle down to the "poorest of the poor" is generally formulated as "reducing unemployment". (This is a far cry from the jubilee ideal of "small individual ownership forever" but there is no escape from translating the jubilee aims into terms of the modern economy).

The real problem remains that those who decide the condoning of the debt have no way of intruding to guarantee that the same economic evils as before would not spring up again; to have this right would give them a power above that of the sovereign state, a thing which is not even to be mentioned. They cannot even demand an exact account of how presumable future loans are to be spent, for the real and immediate benefit of the starving; and such an account even if authorized would be complicated beyond making sense.

7. *Jubilee-inspired systems of helping the poorest to help themselves*

In the last analysis, therefore, the only way to help the poor is to provide incentives and systems, and money, for them to help *themselves*. If they themselves do not wish this strongly and effectively enough -- the way their Jubilee forbears wished small property to be inalienable forever -- then it is hard to see how cancelation of debts will much help those below the lower and lowest income-range.

Neither lowest-level "cooperatives" nor "health and handicap insurance" are hinted in Leviticus 25, though the modern western reader must often feel that their successful recent use is relevant to the unhappy situations being described as needing a Jubilee.

The "Socialist state" in spite of its vilification at its origins and even today (perhaps mostly in the big money circles being invited to cancel their debts) and despite its many still-unsolved weaknesses, has in fact taken steps toward improving the situation of the poor which are now taken completely for granted: health-insurance, job-security. Along with these benefits it has tended to reduce that loyalty and agreed contribution to the success of individual enterprise which was the main merit of the "profit motive".

Since these are the questions which are being currently investigated in every detail and promoted by University departments of sociology and of economics and by secular as well as religious authorities, we must leave the answers to their much greater competence: adding only that what they are trying to do is essentially to translate into modern terms what the Jubilee provisions in their time and situation were envisioning.

8. *Conclusions*

Like all our Bible, the Jubilee chapter of Lev 25 serves its users chiefly for its theological content, and specifically for an ever greater union of the Christian churches hoped fervently by Pope John Paul II. The Christian relevance pivots especially upon the citation of Lev 25,10 via Isa 61,1 by Jesus in the synagogue of Nazareth, Luke 4,18.

The Jubilee is seen proximately as a proclamation, made on a Day of

Atonement implying repentance for ourselves and reconciliation with others. Simultaneously also it is a "celebration of release" which must somehow involve a more just distribution of indebtedness among the poorer populations.

For exegesis the greatest problem of the "seventh year release" and thus also of the Jubilee is how an institution originally intended and formulated to be of help to the poor in the seventh year of each separate case could have been combined into a universal cyclic occurrence. But for today's reverential use of "the Bible as it stands", this no longer constitutes a problem. Nor does the debate whether the Jubilee was anciently at least once really put into practice, or was rather a late-exilic device for regaining the property of returnees to Judah.

The immediate relevance of the Jubilee to the 21st Christian century is its message not to a tiny "chosen people" but to all the inhabitants of the globe. Two-thirds of the world is hungry and in need of "release from its debts; repossession of its land". "The Land is the Lord's" -- to be used for reasonable (even if never perfectly equal) benefit of all people everywhere.

Throughout the Jubilee-chapter and its parallels, the focus is on the small independent farmer and the constant threat of his loss of his property by debt. By "enslaved" farmer is really meant one who having no longer a property of his own must toil as tenant on another's farm. Actually this is the situation of most "peasants" in the world today, especially since the use of very expensive farm-machinery has made private farming no longer economically feasible.

Remedies offered by the Jubilee-chapter to the small farmer as an individual are indeed remote; their benefit is chiefly to his (larger) family, with some religious implications; but most obviously with the economic aim of "entailing" small family-plots inalienably. This cannot be seen as an advantage in today's world; we must offer an equivalent in modern terms.

Western-world solutions like minimum wage and prohibition of child-labor are rejected by the poorer countries as apt to increase rather than diminish the misery-levels. Cancelation of international debts for the poorest countries, constantly implored by Pope John Paul II and already granted by some international banking organizations, must take into account the claims of the original depositors, and in any case will not trickle down effectively to benefit "the poorest of the poor".

In the last analysis, the only foreseeable solution is to give the poorest people incentives and sources to help themselves. This is a problem for University-level researches in economics and sociology, where it is being energetically studied. But efforts like the Jubilee to bring ethics and religion into the picture are still worth our study and reflection.

Epilogue

Our aim in undertaking this volume was not to provide any new or original information, but only to survey what has been added by publications of the last fifty years. But we gradually became aware of two real innovations, perhaps never before investigated, which it may be of interest to mention here.

First is the fact that the Jubilee-chapter does not really aim to provide, unless incidentally, a summary of traditions about social reform and aid to the poor. Its real focus is the independent small farmer. And even this is not for himself as an individual, but for the perpetual inalienability of landed property within the same "important families" who had it "ever since the settlement-days".

Second is the recent research into the spread and nature of "walled" cities, and its repercussion on the actual living conditions of the farmers with whom the Jubilee is concerned. Despite proliferation of villages around 1100 B.C., it has been plausibly maintained that many or indeed most farmers dwelt in the cities, and had to go out quite a distance to begin their tillage. The city-dwelling "(owner)-farmers" would include those who had bought out debt-defaulters (except indeterminably some who may have elected to occupy the foreclosed land to till or supervise it themselves) and the "latifundists". Also included were probably the "hired men" or other aliens. But likely enough the city dwellers were largely the small independent farmers and those reduced by debt to tenancy: in other words the principal focus of the jubilee chapter, so that their lodging-conditions deserve more attention from exegesis.

Bibliography in Alphabetical Order

ABERBACH Moshe, *Labor, Crafts and Commerce in Ancient Israel*. Jerusalem 1994, Magnes. Agriculture p. 4-7.

ALBERTZ Rainer, *A History of Israelite Religion in the Old Testamwent Period* 2 (< Göttingen 1992), tr, John BOWDEN. London 1994, SCM.

ALBRIGHT William F., "The List of Levitic Cities", in *Louis Ginzberg Jubilee Volume*. (New York 1945, American Academy for Jewush Research) 49-72.

ALLIS O.T., "Leviticus" p. 140-162 in *New Bible Commentary Revised*, ed. J.A. MOTYER, *al.* Leicester 1970, Inter-Varsity.

ALLON Gedaliah (Heb.). "The Sociological Method in the Study of Jewish Law", *Tarbiz* 10 (1939) 241-282.

ALT Albrecht, "Der Anteil des Königtums an der sozialen Entwicklung in den Reichen Israel und Juda" < Fest. J. LEIPOLDT 1955, in *Kleine Schriften* 3 (Munich 1959, Beck) 348-372.

ALT Albrecht, "Die Ursprünge des israelitischen Rechts", *Verhandlungen der sächsischen Akademie ph/h* 86,1 (Leipzig 1934); "The Origins of Israelite Law", Eng. by R. A. WILSON 1966 = Biblical Seminar 9 (Sheffield 1989, JSOT Press) 79-132.

AMIT Yairah, "The Jubilee Law -- an Attempt at Instituting Social Justice", in Henning REVENTLOW and Yair HOFFMAN, ed., *Justice and Righteousness; Biblical Themes and their Influence* (Bochum 1990): JSOT.S 137 (Sheffield 1992) 47-59.

ANDREASEN N.E.,"Town & Country in the OT", *Encounter* 42 (1981) 259-275.

ARCHI Alfonso, "The Epigraphic Evidence from Ebla and the Old Testament", *Biblica* 60 (1979) 556-566.

BACCHIOCCHI S., "Sabbatical Typologies of Messianic Redemption", *Journal for the Study of Judaism* 17 (1986) 153-176.

BALTZER K., "Naboths Weinberg (1. Kön. 21). Der Konflikt zwischen israelitischem und kanaanäischem Bodenrecht", *Wort und Dienst* 8 (1965) 73-88.

BARDTKE Hans, "Die Latifundien in Juda während der zweiten Hälfte des achten Jahrhunderts v. Chr. (Jes 5,8-10)", *Hommage à A. DUPONT-SOMMER* (Paris 1971, A. Maisonneuve) 235-254.

BARROIS G.A.,"Debt, debtor",*Interpreter's Dictionary of the Bible* 1 (1962) 309-10.

BARTON John, *Ethics and the Old Testament*. London 1998, SCM. 109 p.

BATTO B.F., "Land Tenure and Women at Mari", *JESHO* 23 (1980) 209-239.

BEN-BARAK Zafrira, "Meribaal and the System of Land-Grants in Ancient Israel", *Biblica* 62 (1981) 73-91.

BEN-GAVRIEL M.Y., "Das nomadische Ideal in der Bibel," *Stimmen der Zeit* 171 (1963) 253-263.

BERGANT Diane, "Jubilee", *The Bible Today* 37 (1999) 342-8.

BESS S.H., *Systems of Land Tenure in Ancient Israel.* Ann Arbor 1963, Univ. Michigan diss. often cited in FAGER.

BIMSON J.J., *Redating the Exodus and Conquest*[2] (Sheffield 1981, Almond) & *Biblical Archaeology Review* 13,5 (1987) 40-53 . 60-88; & 14,4 (1988) 52-55.

BIMSON J.J., "The Origins of Israel in Canaan: an Examination of Recent Theories", *Themelios* 15 (1989) 4-15.

BLENKINSOPP Joseph, "Temple and Society in Achaemenid Judah", in *Second Temple Studies 1*, ed. P. DAVIES: *Journal for the Study of the OT* supp. 117, Sheffield 1991. p. 22-53.

BLUM Erhard, *Studien zur Komposition des Pentateuch* (Diss. Heidelberg 1988): BZAW 189. Berlin 1990, de Gruyter.

BOLING R., "Levitical Cities: Archaeology and Texts", in Fest S. IWRY, *Biblical and Related Studies*, ed. A.KORT, S. MIRSCHAUER (Winona Lake IN 1985, Eisenbrauns) 23-32.

BOROWSKI Oded, *Agriculture in the Iron Age* (diss. Michigan 1979).

BOTTÉRO J., "Désordre économique et annulation des dettes en Mésopotamie à l'époque paléo-babylonienne", *JESHO* 4 (1961) 113-164.

BOTTINI Laura, "Il Giubileo in due autori arabo-cristiani", → ZAPPELLA Marco, *Le origini degli anni giubilari* (Casale Monferrato 1998, Piemme) p.221-238

BRENNER Athalya, *The Israelite Woman; Social Role and Literary Type in Biblical Narrative*: Biblical Seminar 2. Sheffield 1985, JSOT.

BRETTLER Marc, *The Creation of History in Ancient Israel.*London 1995,Routledge.

BRICHTO Herbert C., "Kin, Cult, Land and Afterlife -- a Biblical Complex", *HUCA* 44 (1973) 1-55.

BROWN John Pairman, "Men of the Land and the God of Justice in Greece and Israel", *ZAW* 95 (1983) 376-403.

BRUEGGEMANN Walter, *The Land*: OvertBT 1. Philadelphia 1977 Fortress. xiv-196p.

CARDASCIA G., "Droits cunéiformes et droit biblique": 6th Annual Jewish Studies Congress 1973 (Jerusalem 1976) 63-70.

CARDELLINI Innocenzo, *Die biblischen "Sklaven"-Gesetze im Lichte des keilschriftlichen Sklavenrechts. Ein Beitrag zur Tradition, Überlieferung und Redaktion der alttestamentlichen Rechtstexte*: BonnBB 55. Bonn 1981, Hanstein. xxvii-441 p.

CARDELLINI Innocenzo, "'Possessio' [no] o 'dominium bonorum'? [yes]. Riflessioni sulla proprietà privata e la 'remissa dei debiti' in Levitico 25", *Antonianum* 70 (1995) 333-348.

CARDELLINI Innocenzo, "Le radici del 'Giubileo' biblico", *Seminarium* 39 (1999) 36-62; bibliog. 63-72.

CARMICHAEL Calum, "The Sabbatical/Jubilee Cycle and the Seven Year Famine in Egypt", *Biblica* 80 (1999) 224-239.

CARROLL Robert P., "The Myth of the Empty Land" [Jer 24,6; 29,1-19; ideological contruction of Second Temple period], *Semeia* 59 (1992) 79-93.

CHANEY Marvin, "Ancient Palestinian Peasant Movements and the Formation of Premonarchic Israel", in *Palestine in Transition; the Emergence of Ancient Israel*, ed. D.N. FREEDMAN & D.F. GRAF: Social World of Biblical Antiquity 2. Sheffield 1983, Almond/ASOR. P. 39-90.

CHANEY Marvin L., "Debt Easement in Israelite History and Tradition", in Festschrift N. GOTTWALD, *The Bible and the Politics of Exegesis*, ed. D, JOBLING, *al.* Cleveland 1991, Pilgrim; p. 127-139.

CHARPIN Dominique, "L'*andurarum* à Mari", *MARI* 6 (1990) 253-270.

CHILDE V. Gordon, "The Urban Revolution", *Town Planning Review* 21 (1950) 3-17.

CHILTON Bruce, "Debts", *Anchor Bible Dictionary* 2 (1992) 114-6.

CHIRICHIGNO Gregory C., "The Narrative Structure of Exod 21-23", *Biblica* 68 (1987) 457-479.

CHIRICHIGNO Gregory C., *Debt-Slavery in Israel and the Ancient Near East* (1989 diss.): JSOT supp. 141. Sheffield 1993. 409 p.

CHOLEWIŃSKI Alfred, *Heiligkeitsgesetz und Deuteronomium; eine vergleichende Studie*: Analecta Biblica 66. Rome 1976, Biblical Institute Press. Redaktionskritik Lv 25, p.101-118; Lv 25 und Dt 15, p.217-251.

CLINES David J.A., "Haggai's Temple: Constructed, Deconstructed and Reconstructed" [it was a bank: Rome 1991 SBL meeting], in *Second Temple Studies 2*, ed. T. ESKENAZI: JSOT supp. 175, Sheffield 1994, p. 60-87.

CLINES David J.A. ed. (ELWOLDE John, exec.ed.), "Yobel", *The Dictionary of Classical Hebrew* 4, Y-L. Sheffield 1998, Academic: p. 163.

COGGINS Richard J., "The OT and the Poor", *Expository Times* 99 (1987s) 11-14.

COHEN Mark E., *The Cultic Calendars of the Ancient Near East.* Bethesda MD 1993, CDL-Press. 504 p.

COOGAN Michael D., ed., *The Oxford History of the Biblical World* (13 authors). New York 1998, Oxford Univ. Press. xii-643 p., 25 color (+ 100)

CORTESE Enzo, "L'anno giubilare: profezia della restaurazione ? (Studio su *Lev.* 25)", *Rivista Biblica Italiana* 18 (1970) 395-409.

CORTESE Enzo, "L'esegesi di H (Lev 17-26)", *Rivista Biblica Italiana* 29 (1981) 129-146.

COTTIER Georges, "Réflexions théologiques sur le Jubilé", *Seminarium* 39 (1999) 73-81.

CROSS Frank M. jr., *Canaanite Myth and Hebrew Epic.* Cambridge 1973, Harvard.

CRÜSEMANN Frank, *The Torah* [< *Die Tora* 1992], tr. Allan W. MAHNKE. Edinburgh 1996, Clark. Lev 25, p. 283-6.

DALMAN Gustav H., *Arbeit und Sitte in Palästina.* Gütersloh II. 1932; III. 1935; Bertelsmann.

DAUBE David, *Studies in Biblical Law.* Cambridge 1947, Univ.

DAUBE David, *The New Testament and Rabbinic Judaism* (1956).

DAUBE David, *The Exodus in the Bible.* London 1961, Faber & Faber.

DAVIES Eryl W., "Land: its Rights and Privileges", in *The World of Ancient Israel: sociological, anthropological and political perspectives*, ed. R.E. CLEMENTS. Cambridge 1989, Univ. P. 349-369.

DAVIES Philip R., *In Search of "Ancient Israel":* JSOT supplement 143, Sheffield 1992: Ch.6, "Who Wrote the Biblical Literature. and Where ?"; ch.7, "How Was the Biblical Literature Written, and Why ?"; p. 120 "an exercise in imagination whose purpose is purely heuristic."

DE CHIRICO Leonardo, "The Biblical Jubilee", *Evangelical Review of Theology* 23 (1999) 347-362.

DE GEUS C.H.J., "The Importance of Archaeological Research into the Palestinian Agricultural Terraces, with an Excursus on the Hebrew Word *gbī*", *Palestine Exploration Quarterly* 107 (1975) 65-74.

DE GEUS C.H.J., *The Tribes of Israel. An Investigation into Some of the Presuppositions of Martin Noth's Amphictyony Hypothesis* (diss. Groningen). Assen 1976, van Gorcum. xii-268 p.

DE GEUS C.H.J., "The Profile of an Ancient City", *Biblical Archaeologist* 49 (1986) 224-227.

DE VAUX Roland, *Ancient Israel, its Life and Institutions* [*Les institutions de l'AT* 1958-60], tr. John MCHUGH. London 1969 = 1961, Darton Longmans & Todd. II/11/9, The Jubilee Year, p. 175-7; 8. The Sabbatical Year, p. 173-5; 1. Landed Property, p.164-6; -- II/3, Slaves, p. 80-90; bibliog. for each, p. 532; 525.

DIAKONOFF I.M., "The Rural Community in the Ancient Near East", *JESHO* 18 (1975) 121-133.

DIEPOLD P., *Israels Land*: BWANT 95. Stuttgart 1972, Kohlhammer.

DIETRICH M., also ed., Fest. K. BERGERHOF. *Mesopotamica-Ugaritica-Biblica.* Münster 1993. P. 45-58, "Die Frage nach der persönlichen Freiheit im Alten Orient".

DION Hyacinthe-M., "Yahweh, Dieu de Canaan, et la terre des hommes", *Canadian Journal of Theology* 13 (1967) 233-240.

DOMAR Evsey, ed., *Capitalism, Socialism, and Serfdom.* New York 1989, Cambridge Univ. Press.

EBACH Jürgen, "Sozialethische Erwägungen zum alttestamentlichen Bodenrecht", *Biblische Notizen* 1 (1976) 31-46.

EICHRODT Walther, *Old Testament Theology*, tr. J.A. BAKER. L 1964-7, SCM.

ELLICKSON R.C. & THORLAND C.D., "Ancient Land Law: Mesopotamia, Egypt, Israel", *Chicago-Kent Law Review* 71 (1995) 403 .. < CARMICHAEL C., *Biblica* 80 (1999) 231 n.23.

ELLIGER Karl, *Leviticus*: Handbuch zum Alten Testament 1/4. Tübingen 1966, Mohr/ Siebeck. P. 335-360, Lev 25.

ELLISON H.L., "The Hebrew Slave; a Study in Early Israelite Society", *Evangelical Quarterly* 45 (1973) 30-35.

EMMERSON Grace I., "Women in Ancient Israel", in *The World of Ancient Israel*, ed. R.E. CLEMENTS. Cambridge 1989, Univ. P. 371-394.

EPSZTEIN L., *Social Justice in the Ancient Near East and the People of the Bible.* [< *La justice sociale*, Paris 1983]. London 1986.

ERDMAN Charles R., *The Book of Leviticus, an exposition.* New York 1951, Revell. Jubilee p. 127-133.

EVANS M., *Woman in the Bible.* Exeter 1983, Paternoster.

FAGER Jeffrey A., *Land Tenure and the Biblical Jubilee: a Moral World View.* Ann Arbor 1987, Michigan Univ. diss.

FAGER Jeffrey A., *Land Tenure and the Biblical Jubilee: Uncovering Hebrew Ethics through the Sociology of Knowledge*: JSOT supp. 155. Sheffield 1993. 135 p.

FALEY Roland J., "Leviticus", in *New Jerome Biblical Commentary*, ed. Raymond E. BROWN, *al.* Englewood Cliffs 1990, Prentice-Hall. P. 78 (61-79).

FALK Z.,*Hebrew Law in Biblical Times: an Introduction.* Jerusalem 1964,Wahrmann.

FELIKS J., "Agricultural Methods and Implements in Ancient Erez Israel", *Encyclopaedia Judaica* 2 (1971) 374-382.

FENSHAM F.C., *Exodus*: PredikingOT. Nijkerk 1970, Callenbach. 556 p.

FINET André, "Le 'gage' et la 'sujétion' (*nipûtum* et *kiššatum*) dans les textes de Mari et le Code de Hammurabi", *Akkadica* 8 (1978) 12-18.

FINKELSTEIN J.J., "Some New *misharum* Material and its Implications", *Assyriologische Studien* 16 (1965) 233-246.

FREEDMAN David N. & GRAF David F., *Palestine in Transition; the Emergence of Ancient Israel*: Social World of Biblical Antiquity 2.   Sheffield 1983, Almond/ASOR. 108 p., half by Chaney.

FRICK Frank S., *The City in Ancient Israel* (Princeton diss. 1970): SBL diss. 36. Missoula 1977, Scholars. xiii-283.

FRICK F.S., "Ecology, Agriculture and Patterns of Settlement", in *The World of Ancient Israel: Sociological, Anthropological and Political Perspectives*, ed. R. E. CLEMENTS. Cambridge 1989, Univ. P. 67-93.

FRITZ Volkmar, *The City in Ancient Israel*: Biblical Seminar 29.   Sheffield 1995, Academic. 197 p.; 60 plans.

FUSTEL DE COULANGES Numa D., *The Ancient City, a Study of Religions, Laws and Institutions of Greece and Rome*, tr. W. SMALL. NY 1982, Dillingham.

GAMORAN Hillel, "The Biblical Law against Loans on Interest", *JNES* 30 (1971) 127-134.

GAMORAN Hillel, "The Talmudic Law of Mortgages in View of the Prohibition against Lending at Interest", *HUCA* 52 (1981) 153-165.

GAMORAN Hillel, "Mortgages in Geonic Times in Light of the Law against Usury", *HUCA* 68 (1997) 97-108.

GARCÍA TRAPIELLO J., "Preocupación social en el AT", *Angelicum* 55 (1978) 161-192;.p. 169-171, efforts to help; mostly from DE VAUX.

GELB I.J., "Definition and Discussion of Slavery and Serfdom", *Ugarit-Forschungen* 11 (1980) 283-297 & "Quantitative Evaluation" in Fest. S. KRAMER, AOAT 25 (Neukirchen 1976) 195-207.

GERLEMAN Gilles, "Nutzrecht und Wohnrecht. Zur Bedeutung von *'ḥzh* und *nḥlh*", *ZAW* 89 (1977) 313-325.

GERSTENBERGER Erhard S., *Leviticus*: ATDeutsch 6. Göttingen 1993, Vandenhoeck & Ruprecht. Lev 25: p.337-364.

GIBSON E. Leigh, *The Jewish Manumission Inscriptions of the Bosporus Kingdom*: Texte und Studien zum antiken Judentum 75. Tübingen 1999, Mohr/Siebeck. x-201 p. Lev 25 ‖ p. 62-66.

GINZBERG Eli, "Studies in the Economics of the Bible", *JQR* 22 (1932) 343-408.

GNUSE Robert, "Jubilee Legislation in Leviticus: Israel's Vision of Social Reform", *Biblical Theology Bulletin* 15 (1985) 43-48.

GNUSE Robert K., *You shall not Steal: Community and Property in the Biblical Tradition*. Maryknoll 1985, Orbis. ix-162 p.

GORDON C.H., "Sabbatical Cycle or Seasonal Pattern ?" [on A. KAPELRUD], *Orientalia* 22 (1953) 79-81.

GORDON C.H., "The Biblical Sabbath, its Origin and Observance in the Ancient Near East", *Judaism* 31 (1982) 12-16.

GOTTWALD Norman, *The Tribes of YHWH: a Sociology of the Religion of Liberated Israel 1250-1050 BCE*. London/Maryknoll NY 1979, SCM/Orbis.

GRABBE Lester L., ed., *Can a History of Israel be Written ?* (Dublin 1996 meeting of 20 invited scholars): JSOT supp. 245. Sheffield 1997.

GRAY Mary P., "The *Habiru*-Hebrew Problem in the Light of the Source Material Available at Present", *HUCA* 29 (1958) 135-202.

GRENHOLM Cristina, *The Old Testament: Christianity and Pluralism*: Beiträge zur Geschichte der biblischen Exegese. Tübingen 1996, Mohr-Siebeck. x-293 p. She sees CROATTO (amid BARR, CHILDS, LEVENSON, TRIBLE, VON RAD) as "an approach characterized by perspectivism" but her index does not note jubilee, sabbath, debt, or slavery.

GRUBER Mayer, "The Source of the Biblical Sabbath" [not Babylon], *JANES* 1,6 (1969) 14-20.

HABEL Norman C., *The Land is Mine: Six Biblical Land Ideologies*: Overtures to Biblical Theology (16). Minneapolis 1995, Fortress. xv-190 p.; tables p. 149-157 (Lev 25-27, p. 155-7, middle column).

HAMBURGER H., "Money", *Interpreter's Dictionary of the Bible* 3 (1962) 423-5.

HARRISON Roland K., *Leviticus: an Introduction and Commentary*: Tyndale OT. Leicester 1980. Inter-Varsity. Lev 25. p.223-230.

HARTLEY John E., *Leviticus*: Word Biblical Commentary 4. Dallas 1992, Word. P. 415-488, Lev 25.

HARTMAN Louis F., "Loans", tr. ed. of A. VAN DEN BORN (*Bijbels Woordenboek* [2]1957), *Encyclopedic Dictionary of the Bible*. NY 1963, McGraw-Hill. Col. 1361.

HAUSER Alan J. (& ed.), "Israel's Conquest of Palestine: a Peasants' Rebellion": *JSOT* 7 (1978) 2-19; there 28-34 G.MENDENHALL; 37-52 N. GOTTWALD; 20-27 T. THOMPSON.

HAUSER P.M. & SCHNORE L.F., ed., *The Study of Urbanization*. NY 1965, Wiley.

HEJCL [not Hejel] 1906 Johann, *Das alttestamentliche Zinsverbot im Lichte der ethnologischen Jurisprudenz sowie des altorientalischen Zinswesens*: Biblische Studien 12,1. Freiburg 1906, Herder. 88 p.

HENREY K.H., "Land Tenure in the Old Testament", *PEQ* 34 (1986) 5-15.

HIRSCH S.H., *The Pentateuch* [cited in Gnana ROBINSON, Fest. KOCH p.473].

HOENIG Sidney B., "Sabbatical Years and the Year of Jubilee", *JQR* 59 (Jan. 1969) 222-236.

HOFFNER H.A.jr., *"ybl, y͑bûl"* [< *ThWAT* 3 (1982) 390-3], tr.David E.GREEN], *Theological Dictionary of the Old Testament* 5 (Grand Rapids 1986,Eerdmans)364-6

HOPKINS David C., *The Highlands of Canaan; Agricultural Life in the Early Iron Age* (Vanderbilt diss. 1983): Social World of Biblical Antiquity Series, 3. Sheffield 1985, (JSOT-) Almond. 323 p.; 3 maps.

HORST Friedrich, "Das Eigentum nach dem Alten Testament" [< *Das Eigentum als Problem evangelischer Sozialethik* (Essen 1949, Heft 2 p. 87-102] in his *Gottes Recht, Ges.Stud.* ed. Hans W. WOLFF: Theologische Bücherei 12 (München 1961, Kaiser) 203-221.

HORST F., *Gottes Recht. Gesammelte Studien zum Recht im AT*: Theologische Bücherei 12. Munich 1961, Kaiser.

HORST F., "Zwei Begriffe für Eigentum, *nahalâ* und *"huzzâ"*, in Fest. W. RUDOLPH, *Verbannung und Heimkehr*, ed. A. KUSCHKE (Tübingen 1961, Mohr) p. 135-136.

HOUSTON Walter, "'You Shall Open your Hand to your Needy Brother'; Ideology and Moral Formation in Deut 15:1-18", in J.W. ROGERSON ed., *The Bible in Ethics*: JSOT supp. 207 (Sheffield 1995) 296-314.

HUBBARD Robert L., Jr., "The Go'el in Ancient Israel; Theological Reflections on an Israelite Institution", *Bulletin for Biblical Research* 1 (1991) 1-19.

HUMBERT Paul, *La Terou'a. Analyse d'un rite biblique.* Neuchâtel 1946.

JACKSON B.S., "Biblical Laws of Slavery: a Comparative Approach", in *Slavery and Other Forms of Unfree Labour*. ed. L. ARCHER: History Workshop Series (London 1988, Routledge) 86-101.

JAPHET Sara, "The Laws of Manumission of Slaves and the Question of Relationship between the Collections of Laws in the Pentateuch", in Fest. S.E. LOEWENSTAMM, *Studies in the Bible and Ancient Near East*, ed. Yitschak AVISHUR & Joshua BLAU. Jerusalem 1978, Rubinstein. Eng. vol. p. 199-200 (Heb. vol. 231-250).

JAPHET Sara "The Relation between the Legal Corpora of the Pentateuch in the Light of the Manumission Laws", *Scripta Hierosolymitana* 31 (1986) 63-89.

JAUBERT Annie, "Le calendrier des Jubilés et de la secte de Qumrân. Ses origines bibliques", *VT* 3 (1953) 250-264.

JIRKU A., "Das israelitische Jobeljahr" [< Fest. R. SEEBERG (Leipzig 1929) vol. 2, p. 169-179] in his *Von Jerusalem nach Ugarit.* Graz 1966, Akad. P. 319-329.

JOHNSON Aubrey R., "The Primary Meaning of Root √gō'ēl", *Copenhagen 1953 Congress Volume*: VT.S 1 (1953) 67-77.

JONES A.H.M., "The Urbanization of Palestine" [in Roman times], *Journal of Roman History* 21 (1931) 78-85.

KAHAN Ar., "Economic History", *Encyclopaedia Judaica* 16 (1971) 1266-1324.

KAISER Walter C., Jr., "Leviticus" in *New Interpreter's Bible* ed, Leander J. KECK, 1 (Nashville 1994, Abingdon) p. 985-1191; Lev 25, p. 1116-1175.

KALLAI Zechariah, "The System of Levitic Cities: a Historical-Geographical Study in Biblical Historiography", *Zion* 45 (1980) 13-34 in Hebrew; English p. I-II.

KAMP K.A. & YOFFEE N., "Ethnicity in Ancient Western Asia during the Early Second Millennium B.C.: Archaeological Assessments and Ethno-archaeological Prospectives: *BASOR* 237 (1980) 85-104.

KAPELRUD Arvid S., "The Number Seven in Ugaritic Texts", *VT* 18 (1968) 494-9.

KAPLAN C., Heb. "Studies in the Year of Release and the Jubilee", *Horeb* 6 (1941) 171-187.

KAUFMANN Stephen, "A Reconstruction of the Social Welfare Systems of Ancient Israel", in Fest. G.W. AHLSTRÖM, *In the Shelter of Elyon*, ed. W.B. BARRICK & J.R. SPENCER: JSOT supp. 31 (Sheffield 1984) 279-286.

KIENAST B., "Zum altbabylonischen Pfandrecht", *Zeitschrift der Savigny-Stiftung für Rechtsgeschichte* 83 (1966) 334-8.

KIENAST B., "Bemerkungen zum altassyrischen Pfandrecht", *Welt des Orients* 8 (1975-6) 218-227.

KILIAN Rudolf, *Literarkritische und formgeschichtliche Untersuchung des Heilig-keitsgesetzes* (kath. Diss. Tübingen 1959): BonnerBB 19. Bonn 1963, Hanstein. Lev. 25: 1. Zum Text; 2. Die Schichten: p. 121-130-148.

KINLAW D., "Leviticus", in *Beacon Bible Commentary*. Kansas City 1969, Beacon Hill.

KIPPENBERG H.G., *Religion und Klassenbildung im antiken Judäa. Eine religions-soziologische Studie zum Verhältnis von Tradition und gesellschaftlicher Entwicklung*: Studien zur Umwelt des Neuen Testaments 14. Göttingen 1978, Vandenhoeck & Ruprecht

KLÍMA I., "Im ewigen Banne der *muškēnum*-Problematik", in *Wirtschaft und Gesellschaft im alten Vorderasien*, ed. J. HARMATTA & G. KOMORÓCZY (Buda-pest 1976, Kiadó) 267-274.

KNIGHT G.A.F., *Leviticus*. Edinburgh/Philadelphia 1981, St.Andrews/ Westminster.

KOCH Klaus, *Die Priesterschrift von Exodus 25 bis Leviticus 16. Eine überlieferungsgeschichtliche und literarkritische Untersuchung*: FRLANT 71. Göttingen 1959, Vandenhoeck & Ruprecht.

Koch Klaus, "Sabbatstruktur der Geschichte. Die sogenannte Zehn-Wochen-Apoka-lypse (1 Hen 93,1-1; 91,11-17) und das Ringen um die alttestamentlichen Chronologien im späten Israelitentum", *ZAW* 95 (1983) 403-430.

Kochavi Moshe, "The Israelite Settlement in Canaan in the Light of Archaeological Surveys", *Biblical Archaeology Today*, Jerusalem Congress 1984. Jerusalem 1985, Israel Exploration Society. P. 54-60.

Komoróczy G., "Zur Frage der Periodicität des altbabylonischen *mišarum*", in Fest. I. Diakonoff, *Societies and Languages of the Ancient Near East*, ed. Dandamayev M.A. Warminster 1982, Aris & Phillips. P. 196-205.

Kornfeld Walter, *Studien zum Heiligkeitsgesetz (Lev 17-26)*. Vienna 1952, Herder. 158 p.

Kraeling C.R. & Adams R.M., *The City Invincible: a Symposium on Urbaniza-tion and Cultural Development in the Ancient Near East*. Chicago 1960, Univ.

Kraus F.R., *Ein Edikt des Königs Ammi-ṣaduqa von Babylon*: Studia et Documenta ad Iura Orientis Antiqui Pertinentia 5. Leiden 1958, Brill. xvi-269 p.

Kraus F.R., "Ein Edikt des Königs Samsu-ilumas von Babylon", *Assyriologische Studien* 16 (1965) 225-231.

Kraus F.R., *Vom mesopotamischen Menschen der altbabylonischen Zeit und seiner Welt. Eine Reihe Vorlesungen*: Mededelingen Ned. Akad.; Lett. NR 36,6. Amsterdam 1973, North-Holland. 149 p. (= p. 197-345).

Kraus F.R., *Königliche Verfügungen in altbabylonischer Zeit*: Studia et Documenta ad Iura Orientis Antiqui Pertinentia 11. Leiden 1984, Brill. xx-396 p.

Kugler F.X., *Von Moses bis Paulus*. Münster 1922, Aschendorff.

Kutsch E., "Jobeljahr", *Die Religion in Geschichte und Gegenwart*[3] 3 (Tübingen 1956) 799 [*RGG*[4] 1 (A-B) appeared in 1998].

Lampard Eric, "Historical Aspects of Urbanization", in *The Study of Urbanization* ed. P.M. Hauser & L.F. Schnore (NY 1965, Wiley), p. 521-542.

Landmann Michael, *Messianische Metaphysik*: Jüdische Miniaturen 1. Bonn 1982, Bouvier. "Schmitta und Jowel", p. 79-102.

Lang Bernhard, "The Social Organization of Peasant Poverty in Biblical Israel", *JSOT* 24 (1982) 47-63.

Lang H., "The Jubilee Principle: is it Relevant for Today ?", *Ecumenical Review* 58 (1986) 437-443.

Lapidus I.M., ed. *Middle Eastern Cities: a Symposium on Ancient, Islamic and Contemporary Middle Eastern Urbanism*. Berkeley 1969.

Lasserre Guy, "Luther contre la paupérisation et ses conséquences; lecture rhéto-rique de Dt 15/12-28", *Études Théologiques et Religieuses* 70 (1993) 481-492.

LEGGETT Donald A., *The Levirate and Goel Institutions in the Old Testament, with Special Attention to the Book of Ruth* (diss. Amsterdam 1974). Cherry Hill NJ 1974, Mack. [E. LEVINE critique, *Biblica* 57 (1976) 554-9].

LEHRMAN S. M., "Book of Leviticus", *Soncino Chumash* 1947; ch. 25, p. 764-773.

LEMCHE N.P., "The 'Hebrew Slave': Comments on the Slave Law Ex. xxi 2-11", *VT* 25 (1975) 1-28.

LEMCHE N.P., The Manumission of Slaves -- the Fallow Year -- the Sabbatical Year -- the Jobel Year", *VT* 26 (1976) 38-59.

LEMCHE N.P., "*Andurarum* and *mišarum*: Comments on the Problem of Social Edicts and their Application in the Ancient Near East", *JNES* 38 (1979) 11-22.

LEMCHE N.P., "'Hebrew' as a National Name for Israel", *Studia Theologica* 33 (1979) 1-28.

LEMCHE N.P., "Israel in the Period of the Judges -- The Tribal League in Recent Research", *Studia Theologica* 38 (1984) 1-28.

LEMCHE Neils P., *Early Israel. Anthropological and Historical Studies on the Israelite Society Before the Monarchy*: Vetus Testamentum Supplement 37. Leiden 1985, Brill. xv-496 p.

LEVINE Baruch A., *Leviticus*: Torah Commentary. Philadelphia 1989, Jewish Publication Society.

LEVINE Baruch A., "On the Semantics of Land Tenure in Biblical Literature (Lev 25,10 *ʾhuzzâ*)", Fest. W.W. HALLO, *The Tablet and the Scroll* (Bethesda 1993, CDL) 134-9.

LEVY Thomas, ed., *The Archaeology of Society in the Holy Land*. New York 1995, Facts on File.

LEWY Julius, "The Biblical Institution of *Dᵉrôr* in the Light of Akkadian Documents", *Eretz-Israel* 5 (Fest. B. MAZAR 1958) *21-*31.

LIEBER David L., "Sabbatical Year and Jubilee", *Encyclopaedia Judaica* 14 (1971) 574-577 (-582).

LIM T.H., al., ed., *The Dead Sea Scrolls in their Historical Context*. Edinburgh 1999.

LINDENBERGER James M., "How Much for a Hebrew Slave ? The meaning of *mišneh* in Deut 15:18", *JBL* 110 (1991) 479-482.

LIPIŃSKI Edward, "Sale, Transfer, and Delivery in Ancient Semitic Terminology", in *Gesellschaft und Kultur im alten Vorderasien*, ed. Horst KLENGEL: Schriften zur Geschichte und Kultur des Alten Orients 15. Berlin 1982, Akademie. P. 173-185. [P.235-246: Winfried THIEL, "Soziale Wandlungen in der frühen Königszeit Alt-Israels".]

LIVERANI Mario, "Communautés de village et palais royal dans la Syrie du IIème millénaire", *JESHO* 18 (1975) 146-164.

LORETZ Oswald, "Ugaritisches ṣamātu und hebräisches ṣm(y)tt", *Biblische Zeitschrift* 6 (1962) 269-279.

LORETZ Oswald, "Die prophetische Kritik des Rentenkapitalismus", *Ugarit-Forschungen* 7 (1975) 271-8.

LORETZ Oswald, *Habiru-Hebräer. Eine sozio-linguistische Studie über die Herkunft des Gentiliziums 'ibri vom Appellativum Ḥabiru*: BZAW 160. Berlin 1984, de Gruyter.

MCCONVILLE J.G., *Law and Theology in Deuteronomy* (diss. Belfast 1980): JSOT.S 33. Sheffield 1984. 214 p.

MCKANE W., "Ruth and Boaz", *Glasgow University Oriental Society Transactions* 19 (1962) 29-40.

MCKEATING Henry, "Vengeance is Mine [Rom 12.19]: a Study of the Pursuit of Vengeance in the Old Testament", *Expository Times* 74 (1962-3) 239-245.

MCKEATING Henry, "The Development of the Law of Homicide in Ancient Israel", *VT* 25 (1974) 45-68.

MACKENZIE Roderick A.F., "The Formal Aspect of Ancient Near Eastern Law", in Fest. T.J. MEEK, *The Seed of Wisdom*, ed. W.S. MCCULLOUGH. Toronto 1964, Univ. P. 31-45.

MADARO Paola, "Il Giubileo nell'interpretazione dei Padri Greci", → ZAPPELLA Marco, *Le origini degli anni giubilari* (Casale Monferrato 1988, Piemme) p.185-219; bibliog. 219-220.

MALONEY Robert P., "Usury and Restrictions on Interest-Taking in the Ancient Near East", *CBQ* 56 (1974) 1-20.

MATHYS Felix, "Sabbatruhe und Sabbatfest", *ThZ* 28,4 (1972) 241-262 (fasc. 3 also has duplicated pages 241-256).

MAY Herbert G., "A Sociological Approach to Hebrew Religion", *Journal of Bible and Religion* 14 (1934) 306-329.

MAYER G.,"kesep", *ThWAT* 4 (1982) 283-297 = TDOT 7 (tr. D. GREEN 1995) 270-82

MAZAR Amihai, "The Israelite Settlement in Canaan in the Light of Archaeological Excavations", *Biblical Archaeology Today*, Jerusalem Congress 1984. Jerusalem 1985, Israel Exploration Society. P. 61-71 (-95).

MEINHOLD A., "Zur Beziehung Gott, Volk, Land im Jobel-Zusammenhang", *Biblische Zeitschrift* 29 (1985) 245-261.

MEINHOLD Arndt, "Jubeljahr [sic!; col. 89 sub Jobel gives renvoi to Jubeljahr]", *Theologische Realenzyklopädie* 17 (1988) 280-1.

MENDELSOHN Isaac, *Slavery in the Ancient Near East* (NY 1949, Oxford; and/or same title "BAR 3").

MENDENHALL George, *The Tenth Generation: the Origins of the Biblical Tradition.* Baltimore 1973, Johns Hopkins Univ.

MENES Abram, *Die vorexilischen Gesetze Israels*: BZAW 50 (1928). vii-143 p.

MERENDINO Rosario P., *Das deuteronomische Gesetz. Eine literarkritische, gattungs- und überlieferungsgeschichtliche Untersuchung zu Dt 12-26* (Diss. Bonn 1966): BonnerBB 31. Bonn 1986, Hanstein. Deut 15, pp. 106-124; source-table p.112.

MEZZACASA Florencio, "Esdras, Nehemias y el año sabático", *Revista Bíblica* 23/99 (1961) 1-8 . 82-96.

MILGROM Jacob, "The Levitic Town: an Exercise in Realistic Planning", *Journal of Jewish Studies* 33 (1982) 185-8.

MILGROM Jacob,"The Land Redeemer and the Jubilee", Fest.D.N. FREEDMAN, *Fortunate the Eyes that See*, ed.A. BECK,*al.* Grand Rapids 1995,Eerdmans; p.66-9.

MILLER J. Maxwell & HAYES John H. [not = Hayes-Miller 1977], *A History of Ancient Israel and Judah.* Philadelphia 1986, Westminster.

MIRANDA José Porfirio, *Communism in the Bible.* Maryknoll 1981, Orbis.

MORROW William, "The Composition of Deut 15:1-3", *Hebrew Annual Review* 12 (1990) 115-131.

MUNCH P.A., "Die wirtschaftliche Grundlage des israelitischen Volksbewusstseins vor Saul. Ein Beitrag zur Vorgeschichte Israels", *ZDMG* 92 (1939) 217-253.

NA'AMAN Nadiv, "Habiru and Hebrews; the Transfer of a Social Term to the Literary Sphere", *JNES* 45 (1986) 271-258.

NEGRETTI Nicola, *Il settimo giorno. Indagine critico-teologica delle tradizioni pre-sacerdotali e sacerdotali circa il sabato Biblico* (diss. 1971): AnB 55. Rome 1973, Biblical Institute Press. 341 p.

NELSON Benjamin, *Usura e cristianesimo. Per una storia dell'etica moderna* [The Idea of Usury], tr. Sergio MORAVIA. Firenze 1967, Sansoni.

NEUFELD Edward, "The Rate of Interest and the Text of Neh 5:11" [12%]: *JQR* 44 (1953) 194-204.

NEUFELD Edward, "The Prohibition against Loans at Interest in Ancient Hebrew Laws", *HUCA* 26 (1955) 355-412.

NEUFELD Edward, "Socio-economic Background of Yōbēl and Šᵉmit t ā", *Rivista degli Studi Orientali* (held over from G. FURLANI Festschrift 32) 33 (1958) 53-124.

NEUFELD Edward, "The Emergence of a Royal-Urban Society in Ancient Israel", *HUCA* 31 (1960) 31-53.

NEUFELD Edward, "Inalienability of Mobile and Immobile Pledges in the Laws of the Bible" [only a means of putting pressure on the debtor], *Revue Internationale des Droits de l'Antiquité* 3/9 (1962) 33-44.

NEUSNER Jacob, *School, Court, Public Administration; Judaism and its Institutions in Talmudic Babylonia*: Brown Judaic Studies 83. Atlanta 1987, Scholars.

NICHOLSON E., *The Pentateuch in the Twentieth Century; the Legacy of Julius* WELLHAUSEN. Oxford 1998, Clarendon.

NICOLSKIJ J., "A Nay Buch vegn der Sotsial-Ekonomisher Geshichte fun Folk Yisrael", *Zeitschrift* 2-3 (1928) 165-184; → North R., *Sociology* 1954, p.x.

NODET Étienne, *A Search for the Origins of Judaism, from Joshua to the Mishnah* [*Essai sur les origines du Judaïsme* 1993], tr. E. CROWLEY: JSOT supp. 248 (Sheffield 1997) p. 349.

NORTH Christopher R. [wrongly attributed to R(obert) North by Hartley's p. 416], "The Redeeming God", *Interpretation* 2 (1948) 3-16; p. 5 on *gō'ēl*.

NORTH R.,"The Biblical Jubilee and Social Reform",*Scripture* 4 (1951) 323-335.

NORTH R., "Maccabean Sabbath Years", *Biblica* 34 (1953) 501-515.

NORTH Robert, *Sociology of the Biblical Jubilee*: Analecta Biblica 4. Rome 1954, Biblical Institute Press. xlvi-245 p.

NORTH R., "*Yad* in the Shemitta-Law", *VT* 4 (1954) 196-9.

NORTH R., "The Derivation of Sabbath", *Biblica* 36 (1955) 182-201.

NORTH R., "Flesh, Covering, and Response, Ex. xxi 10", *VT* 5 (1955) 204-6.

NORTH R., "Il latifondo nella Bibbia", *Civiltà Cattolica* 107 (1956, 4) 612-9.

NORTH R., "Jubileo", *Enciclopedía Bíblica* (Barcelona 1963, Garriga) p. 710-711.

NORTH R., *jôbel* [< *ThWAT* 3 (1982)] tr. David E. GREEN, *TDOT* 6 (1990) 1-6 [*deror* 3 (1978) 265-9; *mas* tr. D. W. STOTT, 8 (1997) 427-443].

NORTH R., *Medicine in the Biblical Background and Other Essays on the Origins of Hebrew*: Analecta Biblica 142. Rome 2000, Pontifical Biblical Institute Press. 194 p.

NOTH Martin, *Das dritte Buch Mose, Leviticus*: Altes Testament Deutsch 6. Göttingen 1962, Vandenhoeck & Ruprecht. Lev 25, p. 157-169.

OLIVIER H., "The Effectiveness of the Old Babylonian *Mēšarum* Decree", *Journal of North-West Semitic Languages* 12 (1984) 107-113.

OTTO Eckart, *Theologische Ethik des Alten Testaments*: ThWiss 3,2. Stuttgart 1994, Kohlhammer. "Das Programm der Sozialethik: Der Ausgleich zwischen Arm und Reich durch die Sabbatordnung", p.249-256; bibliog.

OTTO Eckart,"Das Heiligkeitsgesetz.Leviticus 17-26 in der Pentateuchredaktion", Fest H.REVENTLOW. *Altes Testament,Forschung und Wirkung*, ed.P.MOMMER, W.THIEL. Frankfurt 1994 Lang. P.65-80 (mostly on Lev 19; only p. 72 on Lev 25).

OTTO Eckart, "Programme der sozialen Gerechtigkeit. Die neuassyrische *(an-)durāru* Institution sozialen Ausgleichs und das deuteronomische Erlassjahr in Dtn 15", *Zeitschrift für Altorientalische und Biblische Rechtsgeschichte* 3 (1997) 23-63 (64-. 91 . 92-111 *al.*).

PARENTELLI Gladys, "Who Bought God's Land ?" *Latin-American Documentation* 30,2 (1999) 1-18.

PARUZEL H., "La jubilea jaro en la Biblio", *Biblia Revuo* 11 (1975) 7-10.

PAUL Shalom M., *Studies in the Book of the Covenant in the Light of Cuneiform and Biblical Law*: VTS 18. Leiden 1970, Brill. xii-149 p.

PEDERSEN Johannes, *Israel, its Life and Culture*, 1-2 tr. Mrs.Aslang MØLLER; 3-4 tr. Annie L. FAUSBØLL. London 1926-1940. x-579 p.; v-789 p.

PETERSON J.L., *A Topographical Surface Survey of the Levitical Cities of Joshua 21 and 1 Chronicles 6* (diss.) Chicago 1977, Seabury-Western [< CHIRICHIGNO JSOT.S 141 p. 386].

PHILLIPS A., "The Law of Slavery: Exodus 21:2-11", *JSOT* 30 (1984) 51-66.

PORTER J.R., *Leviticus*: Cambridge Bible Commentary. Cambridge 1976, Univ. Lev. 25, p.195-206.

PRICE Barbara J., "Secondary State Formation: an Explanatory Model", in *Origins of the State*, ed. R. COHEN & E.R. SERVICE. Philadelphia 1978, Institute for the Study of Human Issues. P. 161-186.

PROVAN Iain W., "Ideologies, Literary and Critical: Reflections on Recent Writing on the History of Israel", *JBL* 114 (1995) 585-606; rejoinders there by THOMPSON and DAVIES p. 683-698-705.

RABINOWITZ Y., "*Ba'alût*", *Enšiqlopediya Miqra'ît* 2 (Jerusalem 1954) 295-8.

REDMAN Charles L., *The Rise of Civilization: from Early Farmers to Urban Society in the Ancient Near East*. San Francisco 1978, Freeman.

REID Stephen B., "Miller-Hayes as 'Normal Science'". *JSOT* 39 (1987) 41, amid six critiques p. 3-63 (1986 meeting): moderate, but -- "this will be the last of its kind".

REIFENBERG Adolf, *The Soils of Palestine; Studies in Soil Formation and Land Utilization in the Mediterranean*², tr. C.L. WHITTLES. London 1947, T. Murphy.

RENDTORFF Rolf: *Leviticus*: BKAT 3/1. Neukirchen 1985.

RENDTORFF Rolf, *The Old Testament; an Introduction*, tr. J. BOWDEN. Philadelphia 1986, Fortress.

RENDTORFF Rolf, *The Problem of the Process of Transmission in the Pentateuch* (< BZAW 147, 1977) tr. John J. SCULLION: JSOT supp. 89. Sheffield 1990.

RENGER Johannes, "On Economic Structures in Ancient Mesopotamia", *Orientalia* 61 (1994) 157-208.

REVENTLOW Henning G., *Das Heiligkeitsgesetz formgeschichtlich untersucht*: WMANT 6. Neukirchen 1961. 171 p.; Lev 25, p. 123-142.

RINGE Sharon H., *Jesus, Liberation, and the Biblical Jubilee*: OverturesBT 19. Philadelphia 1985. Fortress. xviii-124 p.

ROBINSON Gnana, *The Origin and Development of the Old Testament Sabbath: a Comprehensive Exegetical Approach*: Beiträge zur biblischen Exegese und Theologie 21. Frankfurt 1988, Lang.

ROBINSON Gnana, "Das Jobel-Jahr. Die Lösung einer sozial-ökonomischen Krise des Volkes Gottes", in Fest. K. KOCH, *Ernten, was man sät*, ed. DANIELS D., al. Neukirchen 1991; p.471-494.

ROST Leonard, "Gruppenbildungen im AT" [und Qumran], *TLZ* 80 (1955) 1-7.

ROWTON Michael, "Dimorphic Structure and the Problem of the 'Apirû-'Ibrîm", *JNES* 35 (1976) 13-20.

SANDERS H.,"Jubeljaar en Schemittajaar", *Theologisch Tijdschrift* 46 (1912) 531-540.

SANDERS James A., "From Isaiah 21 to Luke 4", in Morton SMITH Fest., *Christianity, Judaism, and Other Greco-Roman Cults, 1*, ed. J. NEUSNER (Leiden 1975) 75-106.

SANDERS W.T. & WEBSTER D., "Unilineality, Multilineality, and the Evolution of Complex Societies", in *Social Archaeology*, ed. C.L. REDMAN al. New York 1978. Academic. P. 249-302.

SARNA Nahum, "Zedekiah's Emancipation of Slaves [Jer 34,12-16] and the Sabbatical Year", Fest. C.H. GORDON, *Orient and Occident*, ed. H. HOFFNER: AOAT 22. Kevelaer 1973, Butzon & Becker. P. 143-149.

SAYDON P.P., "Leviticus" in *A New Catholic Commentary on Holy Scripture*, ed. R.C. FULLER, al. London 1969, Nelson. Pp. 228-241.

SEELIGMANN I.L., "Lending, Pledge and Interest in Biblical Law and Hebrew Thought" Fest. S. LOEWENSTAMM, *Studies in the Bible and the Ancient Near East* (1978), p.183-206.

SEIDL Theodor, "Jobeljahr", *Lexikon für Theologie und Kirche*[3] 5 (Freiburg 1996, Herder) col. 854-6.

SHIFF Lawrence, "Neo-Babylonian 'Interest-Free' Promissory Notes". *Journal of Cuneiform Studies* 40 (1988) 187-194, citing E. BILGIÇ 1947.

SICRE J.L., *"Con los Pobres de la Tierra". La justicia social en los profetas de Israel*. Madrid 1984, Cristiandad.

SIKKEMA R.K., *De Lening in het Oude Testament*. 's Gravenhage 1957.

SJOBERG Gideon, *The Preindustrial City, Past and Present*. Glencoe IL 1960, Free Press.

SKLBA Richard, "The Redeemer of Israel", *CBQ* 34 (1972) 1-38.

SLOAN Robert B., *The Favorable Year of the Lord: a Study of Jubilary Theology in the Gospel of Luke* (diss. Basel) Atlanta/Fort Worth 1977, Scholars/Schola. x-213 p.

SNAITH N.H., "Leviticus" in *Peake's Commentary on the Bible*, ed. Matthew BLACK & H.H. ROWLEY. London 1962, Nelson. P. 241-253 [p. 137, M. BURROWS on Jubilee].

SOGGIN J.Alberto, "L'anno sabbatico e il Giubileo nella Bibbia": Retirement Lecture, Pontifical Biblical Institute, Nov. 13, 1999 [→ *Acta P.I.B.* 2000].

SOMMER Benjamin D., "Revelation at Sinai in the Hebrew Bible and in Jewish Theology", *Journal of Religion* 79 (1999) 422-451.

SOSS Neal M., "Old Testament Law and Economic Society", *Journal of the History of Ideas* 34 (1973) 323-344; p.337-340, fallow & jubilee.

STAGER Lawrence E., *Ancient Agriculture in the Judean Desert: A Case Study of the Buqeiah Valley in the Iron Age* (diss. Harvard 1975).

STAGER L.E., "Agriculture" in *Interpreter's Dictionary of the Bible supplement*, ed. Keith CRIM. Nashville 1978, Abingdon. P. 11-13.

STAGER L.E., "The Archaeology of the Family in Ancient Israel", *BASOR* 260 (1985) 1-35.

STAGER Lawrence E., "Israelite Settlement in Canaan", in Jerusalem congress *Biblical Archaeology Today*, ed. Amihai MAZAR (Jerusalem 1985, Israel Exploration Soc,) 83-87.

STAGER L.E., "The Impact of the Sea Peoples (1185-1050 BCE)" in *The Archaeology of Society in the Holy Land*. ed. Thomas E. LEVY. (New York 1995, Facts on File) 332-348.

STAGER Lawrence E., "Forging an Identity; the Emergence of Ancient Israel", in *The Oxford History of the Biblical World*, ed. Michael D. COOGAN (New York 1988, Oxford) p.123-173.

STAMBAUGH John E., "Cities", *AnchorBD* 1 (1992) 1031-1048.

STAMM Johann J., *Erlösen und Vergeben im Alten Testament. Eine begriffsgeschichtliche Untersuchung*. Bern 1940, Francke. 148 p.; *gô'el* p.27-44.

STAROBINSKI-SAFRAN E., "Sabbats, années sabbatiques et jubilés. Réflexions sur l'exégèse juive et chrétienne de Lév. 25", *Mélanges É. BRÉGUET* (Genève 1978, Typopress) 37-45.

STEIN S.,"The Laws on Interest in the Old Testament", *Journal of Theological Studies NS* 4 (1953) 161-170.

STONE E., "The Hebrew Jubilee Period", *Westminster Review* 175 (1911) 686-696 [never available to me].

STROBEL August, "Die Ausrufung des Jobeljahrs in der Nazarethpredigt Jesu. Zur *apokalyptischen Tradition Lc* $4_{16\text{-}30}$", in Erich GRÄSSER, al., *Jesus in Nazareth*: BZNW 40 (Berlin 1972. de Gruyter) p. 38-50.

STUHLMUELLER Carroll, *Creative Redemption in Deutero-Isaiah*: Analecta Biblica 42. Rome 1970, Pontifical Biblical Institute.

SUN H.T.C., *An Investigation of the Compositional Integrity of the So-Called Holiness Code (Lv 17-26)*: diss. Claremont 1990 [< HARTLEY comm. p. xxxii].

SZLECHTER Émile, "Le prêt dans l'Ancien Testament et dans les Codes mésopotamiens d'avant Hammourabi", *Revue d'Histoire et de Philosophie Religieuses* 35 (1995) 16-25.

TALMON Shemaryahu, "The 'Comparative Method' in Biblical Interpretation -- Principles and Problems", *Göttingen Congress Volume*: VTS 29 (Leiden 1978, Brill) p. 320-356.

TETTAMANZI Dionigi card., *Anno di grazia, tempo di gioia. Meditazione cristiana sul Giubileo.* Casale Monferrato AL 1999. Piemme.

THIEL Winfried, "Die Anfänge von Landwirtschaft und Bodenrecht in der Frühzeit Alt-Israels", in Adelheid BURKHARDT, al., ed. *Altorientalische Forschungen VII*: Schriften zur Geschichte und Kultur des Alten Orients. Berlin 1980, Akademie; p. 127-141.

THOMPSON Thomas L., "The Joseph and Moses Narratives". in HAYES-MILLER. *Israelite and Judaean History* [*not* Miller-Hayes above]. London 1977, SCM. P. 149-180 . 210-212.

THOMPSON Thomas L., *The Origin Tradition of Ancient Israel, I. The Literary Formation of Genesis and Exodus*: JSOT supp.55. Sheffield 1987.

THOMPSON Thomas L., *The Bible in History: How Writers Create the Past.* New York 1999, Basic.

TROCMÉ André, *Jesus and the Nonviolent Revolution*, tr. Michael H. SHANK & Martin E. MILLER. Scottsdale PA 1973, Herald.

TSEVAT Mattatiahu, "Shemittah und Sinai", *Tel Aviv Journal* (1973) 283-8.

TSEVAT Mattatiahu. "The Hebrew Slave according to Deuteronomy 15:12-18: his Lot and the Value of his Work, with Special Attention to the Meaning of *mišneh*", *JBL* 113 (1994) 587-595.

TURKOWSKI L., "Peasant Agriculture in the Judean Hills", *Palestine Exploration Quarterly* 101 (1969) 21-33 . 101-112.

UCKO P.J. & DIMBLEBY G.W., *The Domestication and Exploitation of Plants and Animals*. Sheffield 1969, Almond.

UFFENHEIMER Benjamin, Heb., "Utopia and reality [*mᵉsî'ût*] in biblical thought", *Shnaton* 4 (1980) 10-26; Eng. XIIIs ["Utopia" includes Shemittah and Jubilee as "practicable parts", but also prophetic anticipations].

UNTERMAN Jeremiah, *From Repentance to Redemption*: JSOT supp. 54. Sheffield 1987.

UNTERMAN Jeremiah, "Redemption (OT)", *Anchor Bible Dictionary* 5 (New York 1992, Doubleday) p. 650-654.

VAN DER PLOEG J.P.M., "Slavery in the Old Testamemt", *Uppsala 1971 Congress Volume*: VTS 22. Leiden 1972, Brill. 73-87.

VAN HOUTEN Christiana, *The Alien in Israelite Law*: JSOT supp.107. Sheffield 1991.

VAN NIEUWENHUIZEN C.A.O., *Sociology of the Middle East; Stocktaking and Interpretation*: Social and Political Studies of the Middle East 1. Leiden 1971, Brill.

VAN SELMS Adriaan, "Die Stad in die Israelitiese voorstellingslewe", *Hervormde Teologiese Studies* 8 (Pretoria 1952) 79-89.

VAN SELMS A., "The Year of the Jubilee, In and Outside the Pentateuch", *Ou Testament Werkgemeenskap* 17 (1975) 74-85.

VAN SELMS A., "Jubilee, Year of", *IDBSupp* (1976) 496-8.

VINK J.G., *Leviticus*: Die Boeken van het Oude Testament 2/1. Roermond 1962, Ronen. Ch. 25, p. 88-95.

VON RAD Gerhard, "The Promised Land and Yahweh's Land in the Hexateuch" [< *Zeitschrift des Deutschen Palästina-Vereins* 66 (1943) 191-204] in *The Problem of the Hexateuch and Other Essays* (< 1966); = Philadelphia/London 1984), Fortress/SCM; p. 191-204.

VON RAD Gerhard, *The Problem of the Hexateuch and Other Essays*, tr. E. DICKEN. New York 1966 (= 1984), McGraw-Hill.

VON WALDOW Eberhard H, "Social Responsibility and Social Structure in Early Israel", *CBQ* 32 (1970) 182-204.

WACHOLDER Ben Zion, "The Calendar of Sabbatical Cycles During the Second Temple and the Early Rabbinic Period", *HUCA* 44 (1973) 153-184; tables 185-196.

WACHOLDER B.Z., "Sabbatical Year", *IDB supp* (1976) 762-3.

WACHOLDER B.Z., "Chronomessianism: the Timing of Messianic Movements and the Calendar of Sabbatical Cycles", *HUCA* 46 (1978) 201-218.

WALLIS G., "Das Jobeljahr-Gesetz, eine Novelle zum Sabbathjahrgesetz", *Mitteilungen des Instituts für Orientforschung* 15 (1969) 337-345.

WEBER Beat,"Vergeltung oder Vergebung? Matthäus 18,21-25 auf dem Hintergrund des 'Erlassjahres'", *ThZ* 50 (1994) 125-151; also his *ZNW* 83 (1992) 161-182.

WEBER Max, "Agrarverhältnisse im Altertum", *Gesammelte Aufsätze zur Sozial- und Wirtschaftsgeschichte*. Tübingen 1924.

WEBER Max, *Ancient Judaism* [1917-20 *Archiv für Sozialwissenschaft*], tr. Hans H. GERTH & Don MARTINDALE. New York 1952, (Glencoe) Free Press.

WEBER Max, *Economy and Society 2*, ed. Guenther ROTH & Claus WITTICH. Berkeley 1978, Univ. California.

WEIL Hermann M., "Gage et cautionnement dans la Bible", *Archives d'Histoire du Droit Oriental* 2 (1938) 171-240.

WEIL H.M., "Exégèse de Jér 23,33-4 et de Job 14,28-33", *Revue de l'Histoire des Religions* 118 (1938) 201-208.

WEINFELD Moshe, *Deuteronomy and the Deuteronomic School* (diss. Jerusalem 1964). Oxford 1972, Clarendon. xviii-467 p.

WEINFELD Moshe, *Social Justice in Ancient Israel and in the Ancient Near East* [< Hebrew 1985]. Jerusalem/Minneapolis 1995, Hebrew Univ./Fortress. "Sabbatical Year and Jubilee", p. 152-178.

WEIPPERT Manfred, *The Settlement of the Israelite Tribes in Palestine; a Critical Survey of Recent Scholarly Debate* [< *Die Landnahme*, FRLANT 92, Göttingen 1967], tr, James D. MARTIN. London 1972, SCM. xx-171 p.

WELTEN Peter, "Erklärt dieses fünfigste Jahr für heilig", *BerlinerTZ* 8 (1991) 121-8.

WENHAM Gordon J., *The Book of Leviticus*: New International Commentary OT 3. Grand Rapids 1979, Eerdmans. xiii-362 p.; Lev 25, p.313-324.

WESTBROOK Raymond, *Property and the Family in Biblical Law*: JSOT supp. 113: ch.2, "Jubilee Laws" & ch. 3 "Redemption of Land", = *Israel Law Review* 6 (1971) 209-225 . 367-375.

WHITELAM Keith W., "Between History and Literature: the Social Production of Israel's Traditions of Origin", *JSOT* (1991,2) 60-74.

WHITELAM Keith W., *The Invention of Ancient Israel; the Silencing of Palestinian History*. London 1996, Routledge.

WHYBRAY R.N., "What do we Know about Ancient Israel ?", *Expository Times* 108 (1996f) 71-74.

WOLF E.B., *Peasants*: Foundations of Modern Anthropology 4. Englewood Cliffs NJ 1966, Prentice-Hall.

WRIGHT C.J.H., "What Happened Every Seven Years in Israel ? Old Testament Sabbatical Institutions for Land, Debtors and Slaves", *Evangelical Quarterly* 56 (1984) 129-138.193-201.

WRIGHT Christopher J.H., *God's People in God's Land: Family, Land, and Property in the Old Testament*. Grand Rapids / Exeter 1990, Eerdmans / Paternoster. xx-284 p.

WRIGHT Christopher J.H., "Sabbatical Year", *AnchorBD* 5 (1992) 857-861.

YARON R., "Redemption of Persons in the Ancient Near East", *RIDA* 6 (1959) 155-176.

YODER John H., *The Politics of Jesus*. Grand Rapids 1972, Eerdmans.

ZAPPELLA Marco, ed. (p. 7-10; 241-272) *Le origini degli anni giubilari. Dalle tavolette in cuneiforme dei Sumeri ai manoscritti arabi del Mille dopo Cristo*. Casale Monferrato 1998, Piemme. 1. Cristina SIMONETTI, Gli editti di remissione in Mesopotamia e nell'antica Siria, p. 11-73; bibliog. 71-3;   2. Francesco BIANCHI, Il Giubileo nei testi ebraici canonici e post-canonici, p.75-132 (sua datazione 113-9); bibliog. 133-7;   3. Georg SCHEUERMANN, Il Giubileo negli autori del Nuovo Testamento. p. 139-180; bibliog. p. 180-2; 4. Paola MADARO,   Il Giubileo nell'interpretazione dei Padri Greci. p. 185-219; bibliog. 219-220;   5. Laura BOTTINI, Il Giubileo in due autori arabo-cristiani, p.221-238; bibliog. 238-9.

ZIMMERLI Walther, "Das 'Gnadenjahr des Herrn'" [< Fest. K. GALLING, *Archäologie und Altes Testament* (1970) 321-332] in his *Studien zur alttestamentlichen Theologie*, Ges.Aufs.2. Theol. Bücherei 51 (München 1974, Kaiser) 222-234.

ZISKIND Jonathan R., "Petrus CUNAEUS [VAN DER KUN, 1586-1638, *De republica Hebraeorum* 1617 (Eng. 1653, fr. 1705) I,1-6] on Theocracy, Jubilee, and the Latifundia", *JQR* 68 (Apr. 1978) p. 235-253).

Same Bibliography in Reverse Order of Dates

SOGGIN 2000 J. A., Sabbatico/Giubileo
CARDELLINI 1999 I.,Radici Giubileo
CARMICHAEL 1999 C.,Sabbatical/Egypt
COTTIER 1999 Georges, Réflexions
DE CHIRICO 1999 L., Biblical Jubilee
GIBSON 1999 E.L., *Jewish Manumission*
LIM 1999 T.H., *al.*, *Dead Sea Scrolls*
PARENTELLI 1999 Gladys, Who Bought
SOMMER 1999 B., Revelation/Sinai
TETTAMANZI 1999 D., *Anno di grazia*
THOMPSON 1999 T.L., *Writers Create*
BERGANT 1999 Diane, "Jubilee"
BOTTINI 1998 L., Giub.AraboCr
CLINES 1998 D., Dict. *yôbel*
COOGAN 1998 M. D.,ed.,Oxford HistBib
MADARO 1998 Paola.Giubileo PP Greci
NICHOLSON 1998 E.,*Pentateuch 20th C.*
STAGER 1998 L.E., Forging an Identity
ZAPPELLA 1998 Marco, ed.,*Origini Giub.*
GAMORAN 1997 H.,Mortgages/Geonic
GRABBE 1997 L.L.,ed., *Can a History?*
OTTO 1997 Eckart,Programme...Dt 15
CRÜSEMANN 1996 Frank, *The Torah*
GRENHOLM 1996 C., OT/Chr/Pluralism
SEIDL 1996 Theodor, Jobeljahr *LTK³*
WHITELAM 1996 Keith W., *Invention*
WHYBRAY 1996 R.N.,What do we Know
BRETTLER 1995 M.Z.,Creation of Hist
ELLICKSON 1995 R.,THORLAND,LandLaw
FRITZ 1995 V., *City in Ancient Israel*
HABEL 1995 Norman C., *Land is Mine 8*
HOUSTON 1995 W.,"Needy" Dt 15:1-18
LEVY 1995 T.,ed.,Archaeology/Society
MAYER 1995 G., *kesep* "silver,money"
MILGROM 1995 Jacob, *Land Redeemer*
PROVAN 1995 Iain W., "Ideologies"
STAGER 1995 L.E.,Impact/Sea Peoples
SZLECHTER 1995 Émile, "Le prêt"
WEINFELD 1995 Moshe, Social Justice
ALBERTZ 1994 R. History of Religion 2

CLINES 1994 D., Haggai's Temple
KAISER 1994 Walter C.,Jr.,Leviticus *NInt*
OTTO 1994a Eckart, *Theologische Ethik*
OTTO 1994b E., *Heiligkeitsgesetz*
RENGER 1994 J.,Economic Struct.
TSEVAT 1994 M.,Slave/*mišneh* Dt 15
WEBER 1994 B., Mt 18/Erlassjahr
ABERBACH 1994 Moshe, *Labor, Crafts*
COHEN 1993 Mark E., *Cultic Calendars*
DIETRICH 1993 M., *Mesopotamica-Ug-B*
FAGER 1993 Jefffrey A., *Land Tenure*
GERSTENBERGER 1993 E.S., *Leviticus*
LASSERRE 1993 Guy, "LUTHER/Dt 15"
LEVINE 1993 B.A., Semantics/Lev 25,10
NODET 1993 Étienne, Origins of Judaism
CHIRICHIGNO 1993 G.C., *Debt-Slavery*
AMIT 1992 Yairah, The Jubilee Law
CARROLL 1992 Robert P., Empty Land
CHILTON 1992 Bruce, "Debts", *Anchor*
DAVIES 1992 Philip R., *In Search*
HARTLEY 1992 John E., *Leviticus*
STAMBAUGH 1992 John E., "Cities"
UNTERMAN 1992 J.Redemption (OT)
WRIGHT 1992 C.J.H.,Sabbatical,*Anchor*
BLENKINSOPP 1991 Joseph, Temple
CHANEY 1991 Marvin L.,Debt Easement
HUBBARD 1991 Robert L., Jr., Go'el
LINDENBERGER 1991 J.M.,*mišneh* Dt 15
ROBINSON 1991 Gnana, Das Jobel-Jahr
VAN HOUTEN 1991 Christiana, *The Alien*
WELTEN 1991 Peter, "Erklärt dieses"
WESTBROOK 1991 Raymond, Property
CHARPIN 1990 Dominique.*andurarum*
FALEY 1990 Roland J., "Leviticus"
MORROW 1990 William, Deut 15:1-3
RENDTORFF 1990 Rolf, *PPP Pentateuch*
SUN 1990 H.T.C., *Holiness Code*
WRIGHT 1990 C., *God's People/Land*
ALT 1989 Albrecht, Ursprünge/Origins
BIMSON 1989 J.J., The Origins of Israel

DAVIES 1989 Eryl W., Land: its Rights
DOMAR 1989 Evsey, ed.,*C/Serfdom*
EMMERSON 1989 Grace I., Women/Israel
FRICK 1989 F.S., Ecology, agriculture
LEVINE 1989 Baruch A., *Leviticus*
ROBINSON 1989 Gnana, ṣabbath
BIMSON 1988 J.J., *Redating the Exodus*[2]
JACKSON 1988 B.S., Biblical Slavery
MEINHOLD 1988 Arndt, Jubeljahr
SHIFF 1988 Lawrence, "Interest-Free"
CHIRICHIGNO 1987 Gregory C.,Ex 21-3
COGGINS 1987 Richard J.,OT and Poor
FAGER 1987 Jeffrey A., *Land Tenure*
NEUSNER 1987 Jacob, *School, Court*
REID 1987 Stephen B., Miller-Hayes
THOMPSON 1987 T.L.,*Origin Tradition*
UNTERMAN 1987 Jeremiah, *Redemption*
DEGEUS 1986 C.H.J., "Ancient City"
EPSZTEIN 1986 L., *Social Justice ANE*
HENREY 1986 K.H., "Land Tenure"
HOFFNER 1986 H.A. jr., "*ybl, yᵉbûl*"
JAPHET 1986 Sara, Legal Corpora
LANG 1986 H., "The Jubilee Principle"
MILLER 1986 J.M.& HAYES J.H.,*Hist*
NA'AMAN 1986 N., Habiru & Hebrews
RENDTORFF 1986 Rolf, *OT Introd*
BACCHIOCCHI 1986 S., "Sabbatical"
BOLING 1985 R., Levitical Cities
BRENNER 1985 Athalya,*Israelite Woman*
GNUSE 1985a Robert,Jubilee Legislation
GNUSE 1985b R.K., *You shall/Property*
HOPKINS 1985 D.C., *Highlands/Canaan*
KOCHAVI 1985 Moshe,Israel Settlement
LEMCHE 1985 N.P., *Early Israel*
MAZAR 1985 A.,Israelite Settlement
MEINHOLD 1985 A.,Zur Beziehung/Jobel
RENDTORFF 1985 Rolf: *Leviticus*: BKAT
RINGE 1985 Sharon H., *Jesus/Jubilee*
STAGER 1985a L.E.,Archaeology/Family
STAGER 1985b Lawrence E.,Settlement
KAUFMANN 1984 Stephen,Reconstruction
KRAUS 1984 F.R., *Königliche Verfüg.*
LEMCHE 1984 N.P.,Israel/Tribal League

LORETZ 1984 O.,Habiru-Hebräer BZAW
MCCONVILLE 1984 J.G., *Law/Theol/Dt*
OLIVIER 1984 H.,Effective/*Mēšarum*
PHILLIPS 1984 A.,Law/Slavery: Ex 21
SICRE 1984 J.L., *Con los Pobres*
VONRAD 1984 Gerhard, Promised Land
WRIGHT 1984 C.J.H.,What/Every Seven
BROWN 1983 J.P.,Men/Land/Justice
CHANEY 1983 Marvin,Ancient/Peasant
EVANS 1983 M., *Woman in the Bible*
FREEDMAN 1983 D.&GRAF D.,*Pal/Trans*
KOCH 1983 Klaus,Sabbatstruktur 1Hen
GORDON 1982 C.H., Biblical Sabbath
KOMORÓCZY 1982 G., Zur/Periodicität
LANDMANN 1982 Michael, *Messianische*
LANG 1982 B.,Social Organiz/Poverty.
LIPIŃSKI 1982 Edward, Sale, Transfer
MILGROM 1982 Jacob, Levitic Town
ANDREASEN 1981 N.E.,Town & Country
BEN-BARAK 1981 Zafrira, Meribaal
CARDELLINI 1981 I.,*Bibl."Sklaven"*
CORTESE 1981 Enzo,L'esegesi di H(Lev)
GAMORAN 1981 H., Talmudic/Mortgage
KNIGHT 1981 G.A.F., *Leviticus*
MIRANDA 1981 J.Porfirio, *Communism*
BATTO 1980 B.F.,Land/Women at Mari
GELB 1980 I.J.,Definition/Serfdom
HARRISON 1980 R.K.,*Leviticus/IntComm*
KALLAI 1980 Z.,System/Levitic Cities
KAMP 1980 K.& YOFFEE N., Ethnicity
THIEL 1980 W.,Anfänge/Landwirtschaft
ARCHI 1979 A.,Epigraphic/Ebla/OT
BOROWSKI 1979 O.,*Agriculture/Iron Age*
GOTTWALD 1979 N., *Tribes of YHWH*
LEMCHE 1979a N.P.*Andurarum/mišarum*
LEMCHE 1979b N.P.,'Hebrew' as Israel
WENHAM 1979 Gordon J.,*Leviticus* NInt
BARTON 1978 John, Ethics and OT
FINET 1978 André, 'Gage' et 'sujétion'
GARCÍA TRAPIELLO 1978 J.,Preocupación
HAUSER 1978 A.J.(& ed.), Isr/Conquest
JAPHET 1978 Sara,Laws of Manumission
KIPPENBERG 1978 H.,*Rel/Klassenbildung*

PRICE 1978 Barbara J., Secondary State
REDMAN 1978 C.,*Rise of Civilization*
SANDERS1978 W.&WEBSTER,Unilineality
SEELIGMANN 1978 I.L., Lending, Pledge
STAGER 1978 L.E.,"Agriculture" *IDB*
STAROBINSKI-SAFRAN 1978 E.,Sab/Jub
TALMON 1978 S.,'Comparative Method'
WACHOLDER 1978 B.,Chronomessianism
WEBER 1978 Max,Economy & Society 2
ZISKIND 1978 J.R.,CUNAEUS,*Latifundia*
BRUEGGEMANN 1977 Walter, *The Land*
FRICK 1977 F.S.,*City in Ancient Israel*
GERLEMAN 1977 Gilles, Nutz/Wohnrecht
PETERSON 1977 J.L.,*Topog/LevC/Jos 21*
SLOAN 1977 Robert B., *Favorable Year*
THOMPSON 1977 T. L., Joseph & Moses
CARDASCIA 1976 G., Droits cunéiformes
CHOLEWIŃSKI 1976 Alfred, *H und Deut*
DE GEUS 1976 C.H.J., *Tribes of Israel.*
EBACH 1976 Jürgen, Soz./Bodenrecht
KIENAST 1976 B.,Bemerk./Pfandrecht
KLÍMA 1976 I.,Im ewigen/*muškēnum*
LEMCHE 1976 N.P., Manumission/Jobel
PORTER 1976 J.R.,*Leviticus*: CambridgeB
ROWTON 1976 M., Dimorphic/'Apiru
VAN SELMS 1976 A., Jubilee, *IDBSupp*
WACHOLDER 1976 B.Sabbatical,*IDBsupp*
DEGEUS 1975 C.H.J.,Imp/Agr/Terraces
DIAKONOFF 1975 I.M., Rural Community
LEMCHE 1975 N.P.,'Hebrew Slave'Ex 21
LIVERANI 1975 Mario,Communautés/Syr.
LORETZ 1975 O.,Proph/Rentenkapital.
MCKEATING 1975 Henry, Development
PARUZEL 1975 H., Jubilea jaro/la Biblio
SANDERS 1975 J., From Isa 21 to Lk 4
STAGER 1975 L.E., *Ancient Agriculture*
VANSELMS 1975 A.,Year of the Jubilee
LEGGETT 1974 Donald A., *Levirate/Goel*
MALONEY 1974 Robert P.,"Usury ANE"
ZIMMERLI 1974 W., Gnadenjahr <1970
BRICHTO 1973 H., Kin/Land/Afterlife
CROSS 1973 Frank M., *Canaanite Myth*
ELLISON 1973 H.L., The Hebrew Slave

KRAUS 1973 F.R.,*Vom mesop. Menschen*
MENDENHALL 1973 G., *Tenth Generation*
NEGRETTI 1973 Nicola, *Settimo giorno*
SARNA 1973 Nahum, Zedekiah's/Slaves
SOSS 1973 Neal M., OT Law & Econ.
TROCMÉ 1973 André, *Jesus/Nonviolent*
TSEVAT 1973 Mattatiahu,Shemittah/Sinai
WACHOLDER 1973 BCalendar/Sabbatical
DIEPOLD 1972 P., *Israels Land*: BWANT
MATHYS 1972 Felix, Sabbatruhe/fest
SKLBA 1972 Richard, Redeemer of Isr
STROBEL 1972 A.,Ausrufung/Jobeljahrs
VANDERPLOEG 1972 J.P.M.,Slavery OT
WEINFELD 1972 Moshe, *Deut/School*
YODER 1972 John H., *Politics of Jesus*
BARDTKE 1971 Hans,Latifundien in Juda
FELIKS 1971 J., Agricultural/Israel
FENSHAM 1970 F,C.,*Leviticus*:Prediking
GAMORAN 1971 H.,Bibl/Loans/Interest
KAHAN 1971. Ar., "Economic History"
LIEBER 1971 David L., Sabbatical/Jub
VANNIEUWENHUIZEN 1971 C.,*Sociology*
WEIPPERT 1971 Manfred, *The Settlement*
ALLIS 1970 O.T., Leviticus, *NewBComm*
CORTESE 1970 Enzo, L'anno giubilare
PAUL 1970 S.M.,*Studies/Book Covenant*
STUHLMUELLER 1970 C.*Creative Redemp*
VON WALDOW 1970 E. Soc/Respons/Str
HOENIG 1969 Sidney B.,Sabbatical/Jub
KINLAW 1969 D.,Leviticus,*BeaconBCom*
LAPIDUS 1969 I.M., *Middle E. Cities*
MERENDINO 1969 Rosario P., *Dt 12-26*
SAYDON 1969 P.P.,Leviticus, *NewCathC*
TURKOWSKI 1969 L.,Peasant Agriculture
UCKO 1969 P.& DIMBLEBY G., *Domest*
WALLIS 1969 G.,Das Jobeljahr/Novelle
KAPELRUD 1968 Arvid S.,Number Seven
DION 1967 Hyacinthe,Yahweh/Canaan
NELSON 1967 Benjamin, *Usura*
ELLIGER 1966 Karl, *Leviticus*: HAT
JIRKU 1966 A.,Isr.Jobeljahr < 1929
KIENAST 1966 B.,Zum altbab.Pfandrecht
VON RAD 1966 G. Problem of Hexateuch

WOLF 1966 E.B., *Peasants*: Anthrop.4
BALTZER 1965 K., Naboths Weinberg
FINKELSTEIN 1965 J.J.,Some *misharum*
HAUSER 1965 P.& SCHNORE L.,*Stud.Urb*
KRAUS 1965 F.R.,Edikt Samsu-ilumas
LAMPARD 1965 Eric,Historical/Urbaniz.
EICHRODT 1964 Walther, *OT Theology*
FALK 1964 Ze'ev, *Hebrew Law*
MACKENZIE 1964 R.A.F.,Formal/NELaw
BEN-GAVRIÊL 1963 M.Y., Nomad:Ideal
BESS 1963 S.H., *Systems of Land Tenure*
HARTMAN 1963 Louis F., tr.ed.,Loans
KILIAN 1963 Rudolf, *Literarkritische/H*
NORTH 1963 R., Jubileo, *EncGarriga*
BARROIS 1962 G.A., "Debt, debtor",*IDB*
HAMBURGER 1962 H., "Money", *IntDB*
HIRSCH 1962 S.H.,The Pentateuch [cited]
LORETZ 1962 Oswald, Ug.*samātu*
MCKANE 1962 W., Ruth and Boaz
MCKEATING 1962 Henry, Vengeance
NOTH 1962 Martin, *Leviticus*: ATD
SNAITH 1962 N.H.,Leviticus: *PeakeCom*
VINK 1962 J.G., *Leviticus*: BoekenOT
BOTTÉRO 1961 J., Désordre/des dettes
DAUBE 1961 David, *Exodus in the Bible*
DE VAUX 1961 Roland, *Ancient Israel*
HORST 1961a F.,*Gottes Recht: GesSt*
HORST 1961b, Zwei Begriffe/Eigentum
MEZZACASA 1961 F., Esdras/sabático
REVENTLOW 1961 H., *Heiligkeitsgesetz*
GRUBER 1960 Mayer, Source/Sabbath
KRAELING1960C.&ADAMS,CityInvincible
KUTSCH 1960 E., Jobeljahr, *RGG³*
NEUFELD 1960 E.,.Emerg./Royal-Urban
SJOBERG 1960 Gideon,*Preindustrial City*
ALT 1959 A., Anteil/Königtums/sozial
KOCH 1959 K., *Priesterschrift/Lev 16*
ROST 1959 L.,Gruppenbildungen im AT
YARON 1959 R.,Redemption of Persons
GRAY 1958 Mary P., *Habiru*-Hebrew
KRAUS 1958 F.R.,*Edikt Ammi-saduqa*
LEWY 1958 Julius,Bibl.*Dᵉrôr*/Akkadian
NEUFELD 1958 E.,Soc/ec Yobel/Šemittâ

SIKKEMA 1957 R.K.,*Lening in het OT*
DAUBE 1956 David,*NT/Rabbinic Judaism*
NORTH 1956 R.,Latifondo nella Bibbia
NEUFELD 1955 E., Prohibition/Interest
NORTH 1955a R. Derivation of Sabbath
NORTH 1955b R.,Flesh,Covering: Ex 21
NORTH 1954a R., *Sociology/Bibl.Jubilee*

**Works before 1954 cited here
or previously overlooked**

NORTH 1954b R.,*Yad* in Shemitta-Law
GORDON 1953 C.H.,Sabbatical/Seasonal?
JAUBERT 1953 A.,Calendrier/Jub/Qumran
JOHNSON 1953 A.R., Primary / √*gō'ēl*
NEUFELD 1953 E.,Rate of Interest Neh
NORTH 1953 R.,MaccabeanSabbathYears
STEIN 1953 S., Laws on Interest in OT
KORNFELD 1952 W.,*Stud/H (Lev 17-26)*
VAN SELMS 1952 Adriaan, Stad/israelit.
WEBER 1952 Max,*Ancient Judaism*<1920
ERDMAN 1951 Charles R., *Leviticus*
NORTH 1951 R.,Bibl.Jubilee & Soc.Ref.
CHILDE 1950 V. G., Urban Revolution
HORST 1949 Friedrich, Eigentum AT
MENDELSOHN 1949 Isaac, *Slavery ANE*
DAUBE 1947 D., Studies in Biblical Law
LEHRMAN 1947 S., Leviticus, *Soncino*
REIFENBERG 1947 Adolf, Soils/Palestine
HUMBERT 1946 P., *Terou'a*
ALBRIGHT 1945 W.F., Levitic Cities
NORTH 1945 C!, The Redeeming God
KAPLAN 1941 C.,Heb Stud.Release/Jub
STAMM 1940 J.J.,*Erlösen/Vergeben AT*
ALLON 1939 G.Heb, Sociological/Law
MUNCH 1939 P.A., Wirtsch.Grundlage
WEIL 1938a Hermann M., Gage
WEIL 1938b H.M.,Exégèse Jér 23/Job
DALMAN 1935 Gustav H., *Arbeit/Sitte*
GINZBERG 1932 E., Studies/Economics

JONES 1931 A.H.M.,Urbanization/PalR
MENES 1928 A.,*Vorexilischen Gesetze*
NICOLSKIJ 1928 J., Sotsial-Ekonomisher
MAY 1926 H.G.,Sociological Approach
PEDERSEN 1926 Johannes,*Israel/culture*

WEBER 1924 Max, Agrarverhältnisse
SANDERS 1912 H.,Jubel/Schemittajaar
STONE 1911 E.,Hebrew Jubilee Period
HEJCL 1906 Johann, *AT Zinsverbot*
FUSTEL DE COULANGES 1882 N,*AncCity*

Index of Authors Cited

Scripture Citations

Genesis

-: 107
8,16: 6
12,24: 69
20,16: 54
34,12: 68n29
39-43: 61
40,13: 23
41,44-55: 22
45,1-15: 23
47,18-27: 22
47,18: 23
47,22: 23
47,26: 23
50,15-21: 23

Exodus

-: 64 107 113
3,7: 63
9,13: 15
12,2: 10 14
20,11: 28
21 - Num 10: 99
21-23: 24n9 99
21: 19 60 65 70 81 114
21,1-11: 46n11
21,2: 24 61 64
21,2-11: 60n1 62 67n28
21,2-6: 119
21,3: 111
21,3-6: 69
21,5: 69
21,6: 24,69
21,7: 67 70
21,8: 68
21,9: 69
21,10-11: 69
22,15: 68n29
22,24: 50 51 54
22,25-26: 54
23: 19 36n6 81 114
23,10: 95
23,10-11: 119
23,10-12: 24
23,11: 17 23 30 36 64n12 110 111
23,12: 64

Leviticus

8-13: 112
10: 94n6
16: 10
17-26: 49 86n4 101 103 119
18,3: 23
23,24: 12n7

25 -translation 87-91 98 99
25 -sources: 86 91-94 96 98

25: 15 17 18 22 23 24n10 33n 36 41 43 50 60 68 70 74 79 81 83 94 99 102 112 116 119 125

25-26: 101
25,1: 101
25,1-22: 85n2
25,2: 110 116
25,3: 27
25,3-5: 23
25,4.5: 29n26
25,4: 25n11 30 63
25,6: 23
25,6-13: 10
25,7: 17
25,8: 24 31
25,8-13: 4 18 114
25,8-14: 92
25,8-17: 26n18
25,8-55: 64
25,9: 14 23 32 91 141
25,9-17: 19
25,10: 9 12 17 24 26 31 33n1 47 80 99 113 117 126
25,11: 27
25,13: 11 80
25,13-16: 10
25,14: 43 80
25,14-17: 112
25,15: 119
25,16: 93-94

25,17: 18
25,20: 31
25,20-22: 26 116
25,21: 14 36
25,22: 13 14 31
25,23: 11 33 35 44 64n12 102 110
25,23-55: 85n2
25,26: 12
25,28-31: 91
25,29: 79 80
25,29-34: 73 78
25,30: 64n12 89
25,32: 84
25,32-34: 82
25,33: 46
25,34: 23
25,35: 89
25,35-38: 49 50 51 57 110
25,36: 50 54
25,37: 50 55 110 114
25,39: 80
25,39-46: 112
25,39-55: 66n22
25,40: 24n9 46n11
25,42: 23
25,44: 60
25,45: 80
25,47: 111
25,47-53: 112
25,47-55: 45
25,53: 46n11
25,54: 112
25,55: 23

26: 36
26,3-5: 23
26,4.20: 15
26,34: 25
26,35: 101
26,40: 47
26,46: 101
27: 36
27,17: 113
27,17-24: 23

Numbers

18,20: 82
35,2-4: 82
36,4: 113
36,62: 83

Deuteronomy

-: 64 113
8,8: 29
10,9: 83
15: 19 24 37 60 70 81 95 99 104 111 114
15,1: 64
15,1-18: 55n14
15,1-3: 24 63n9
15,2: 24 63
15,3: 53
15,4: 119
15,4-14: 25
15,4-6: 64n12
15,7-11: 119
15,9: 25 30
15,11: 24n9
15,12: 64
15,12-18: 46n11 62 65n19,21
15,13: 65
15,17: 24 68 69
15,18: 65n20
22,11: 29
23: 19 99
23,20: 50 51 52 55 57
23,21: 51 53
23,22: 54
25,5: 47
32,14: 29

Joshua

-: 12n7 15 18 36n6 37 73 81 99
21: 79 84 143
21,1-42: 82
21,2: 82

Judges

1,7: 10
3,8: 10
4,2: 10
9,5: 47

Ruth

-: 44n5 46n10 111
3,13: 47
4-29: 6

Index of Subjects and Semitic Terms

Finito di stampare
nel mese di aprile 2000

presso la tipografia
"Giovanni Olivieri" di E. Montefoschi
00187 Roma - Via dell'Archetto, 10,11,12